THE TIMELESS CREED OF THE CATHOLIC CHURCH

AS EXPRESSED BY SACRED SCRIPTURE, CHURCH COUNCILS, ROMAN PONTIFFS, FATHERS OF THE CHURCH, AND DOCTORS OF THE CHURCH

ACCOMPANIED BY IMAGES OF SACRED ART, CHURCH HISTORY AND NATURAL WONDERS

Baelena Books

Nihil Obstat:
Reverend Rodney Nootebos
Censor Librorum

Imprimatur:
Most Reverend J. Michael Miller, CSB
Archbishop of Vancouver
April 6, 2016

The *Nihil Obstat* and *Imprimatur* are official declarations that a book or pamphlet is free of doctrinal or moral error. No implication is contained therein that those who have granted the *Nihil Obstat* or *Imprimatur* agree with the contents, opinions or statements expressed.

PUBLISHED BY BAELENA BOOKS
5658 MARLATT AVENUE
POWELL RIVER, BC, V8A 4E7
Editor: Barbara Fiorentino
baelena.mmerlino.com

The Baelena Books logo is taken from a tenth century mosaic of the Basilica Hagia Sophia, Divine Wisdom. In the mosaic, the Emperor Justinian is offering the Church he built to the Mother of God. It has been one of the most influential examples of Christian architecture and is listed as a World Heritage site by UNESCO.

Cover image: Fourth century Christogram, a visual profession of faith in Jesus as Christ. *X* and *P* are the first two Greek letters in the word Christ. The Greek Letters *A* and *ω* represent Christ's words: "I am the Alpha and the Omega, the first and the last, the beginning and the end. Blessed are they who wash their robes so as to have the right to the tree of life and enter the city through its gates." (Rev 22:13-14)

Photo source: Sousse Museum, Sousse, Tunisia   Taken by Mark Merlino, 2006

Scripture texts in this work are taken from the New American Bible, revised edition © 2010, 1991, 1986, 1970 Confraternity of Christian Doctrine, Washington, D.C. and are used by permission of the copyright owner. All Rights Reserved. No part of the New American Bible may be reproduced in any form without permission in writing from the copyright owner.

Copyright © 2016 by Mark Merlino
All rights reserved. No part of this publication may be reproduced without prior permission.
Legal Deposit: National Library of Canada, Ottawa

Merlino, Mark, author, 1979-
The Timeless Creed of the Catholic Church : As Expressed by Sacred Scripture, Church Councils, Roman Pontiffs, Fathers of the Church, and Doctors of the Church / Mark Merlino.

(Catholicism, creeds, Catholic heritage)
Includes bibliographic references and index.
Issued in print format.
ISBN: 978-0-9951731-0-1 (bound)

    1. Catholic Church - - Creeds to 21st century. 2. Christianity Creeds - - Confessions of faith.
3. Cultural Heritage of the Church - - 21st century.   I. Title.

BT993.2   238.11   2016

TABLE OF CONTENTS

Abbreviations..iv

Glossary...iv

Introduction..v

THE PROFESSION OF FAITH

I Believe..1

In one God the Father all powerful, maker of all things both seen and unseen............13

And in one Lord Jesus Christ...43

And in the Holy Spirit..59

In One, Holy, Catholic and Apostolic Church..69

The forgiveness of sins, the resurrection of the body, and life everlasting. Amen........91

APPENDIX

Image References..111

Online Source Databases...113

References to Sacred Scripture..113

References to Ecclesiastical Documents..114

Sacred Art and Photo Index...117

Subject Index...120

Abbreviations

Ap	Apostolic
Bl.	Blessed
c.	Century
CCC	*Catechism of the Catholic Church.* (11 October 1992)
St.	Saint

Glossary of Terms

Creed — A confession, symbol or statement of the Christian faith. The principal Creeds are the Apostle's Creed and the Nicene Creed.

Doctor of the Church — A person who has been declared by the Pope or by a general Ecumenical Council to be of eminent learning and a high degree of sanctity. The Catholic Church recognizes thirty-six people as Doctors of the Church.

Ecumenical Council — A legally recognized meeting of Church leaders and theological experts to discuss matters related to Church doctrine and discipline. The Catholic Church recognizes the validity of twenty-one Ecumenical Councils.

Fathers of the Church — Influential Christian theologians who lived during the first eight centuries of Christianity, generally before the Second Council of Nicaea in 787 AD.

Natural Wonder — Unique or noteworthy place of natural habitat or natural landmarks. UNESCO has declared many places of natural significance as World Heritage sites.

Papal Writings — Extraordinary universal declarations made by Popes as well as ordinary official correspondence addressed to the faithful.

Sacred Art — Fine arts that are oriented towards the infinite beauty of God. Sacred Art both praises God and turns the minds of its viewers devoutly towards God. Sacred Art forms part of the Cultural Heritage of the Church and many examples of Sacred Art have been declared World Heritage by UNESCO.

Sacred Scripture — The Word of God consigned to writing under the inspiration of the Holy Spirit. Along with Sacred Tradition, Sacred Scripture forms one Sacred deposit of the Word of God committed to the Church. The Holy Bible contains 73 separate books divided into the Old Testament and New Testament.

INTRODUCTION

The Timeless Creed of the Catholic Church is intended to be read meditatively. It is a written and visual presentation of what Catholics believe with quotations taken from Sacred Scripture, Ecumenical councils, Papal writings, and the writings of the Fathers and Doctors of the Church. Alongside these quotations, complimentary images of Sacred Art, Church History and Natural Wonders have been placed to visually embody the beliefs described.

By exploring the timeless and living faith of the Church, I have sought the Church's answer to the question, 'What does the Creed mean?'

The Church has adopted the Apostle's and Nicene Creeds as a Symbol of the Faith and the sign and badge of the Christian (Pius XII, Mediator Dei, 47, 20 November, 1947).

Over the centuries, the Church has explained the meaning of its 'Symbol of Faith' through its commentaries on Sacred Scripture, proceedings of Church Councils, Papal documents and by naming certain insightful saints as Doctors of the Church in order to recommend their spiritual writings. Alongside the written Tradition, Sacred Artists and builders have also made manifest the faith through works of beauty, preserving church history, church heritage and capturing wonders found in nature. In compiling this work, I have done nothing other than draw upon and highlight the wealth found in the Catholic tradition.

Preparing *The Timeless Creed of the Catholic Church* has been a pleasure for me and it can best be described by the following quote from the Prophet Isaiah:

> "I am confident and unafraid. My strength and my courage is the Lord, and he has been my savior. With joy you will draw water at the fountain of salvation, and say on that day: Give thanks to the Lord, acclaim his name; among the nations make known his deeds, proclaim how exalted is his name."
>
> (Isaiah 12:2-4)

23 October 2015, Powell River, Canada.

MARK MERLINO

Master of History and Cultural Heritage of the Church
Pontifical Gregorian University

I believe

— The Apostles' Creed

The Apostles' Creed is the ancient baptismal symbol of the Church of Rome... It is "the Creed of the Roman Church, the See of Peter the first of the apostles, to which he brought the common faith"

— CCC, 194

A carpet made of arranged flowers in devotion for the procession of the feast of Corpus Christi in Spello, Italy, 2013.

THE ART OF DEVOTION

The painter Pausias wanting to make drawings of Glycera's different bouquets was unable to do so, as he could not match his skill in painting to the profusion of bouquets she had prepared. In the same way, the Holy Spirit inspires and sets out the teaching on devotion in such a great variety, presenting it through the words and writings of his servants. While the doctrine is always one and the same, yet the compositions in which it is set out are very different according to the variety of ways used in putting them together.

— *St. Francis de Sales, 1609*

Replica of the Spanish ship the Santa Maria used by Christopher Columbus. In 1492, Columbus followed his conviction and sailed into the unknown, proving that the world is a sphere and not flat, 1907.

THE COURAGE TO SEEK

Ask and it will be given to you; seek and you will find; knock and the door will be opened to you. For everyone who asks, receives; and the one who seeks, finds; and to the one who knocks, the door will be opened.
— *Matthew 7:7-8*

What I believe not to exist, I seek not.
— *St. Augustine, 391*

Ever since the creation of the world, his invisible attributes of eternal power and divinity have been able to be understood and perceived in what he has made.

— *Romans 1:20*

THE SUBTLE BEAUTY OF CREATION

Picture of a snowflake taken from under a microscope by Wilson Bentley, 1902, revealing its otherwise hidden symmetry and beauty.

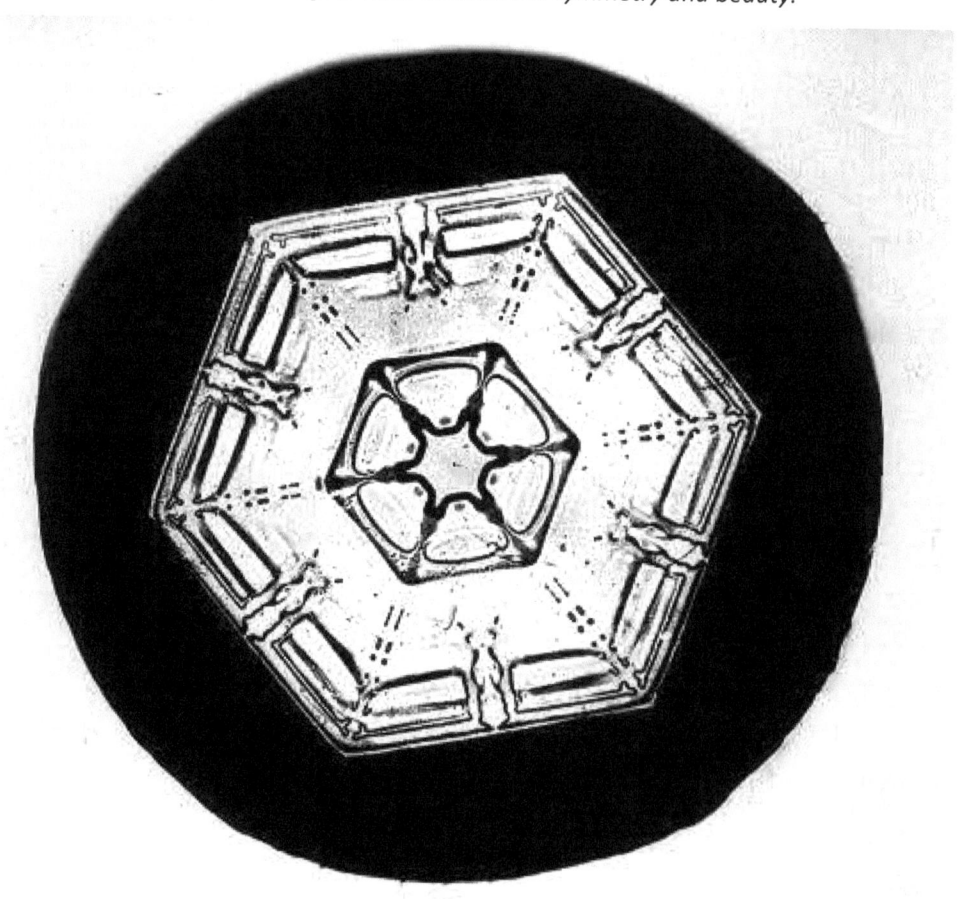

If methodical investigation within every branch of learning is carried out in a genuinely scientific manner and in accord with moral norms, it never truly conflicts with faith, for earthly matters and the concerns of faith derive from the same God. Indeed whoever labors to penetrate the secrets of reality with a humble and steady mind, even though he is unaware of the fact, is nevertheless being led by the hand of God, who holds all things in existence, and gives them their identity.

— *Gaudium et spes, 1965*

INVESTIGATING THE SECRETS OF CREATION

Photo of the Aurora Australis taken from the International Space Station, 2010. The Space Station is a unique laboratory of scientific research and exploration.

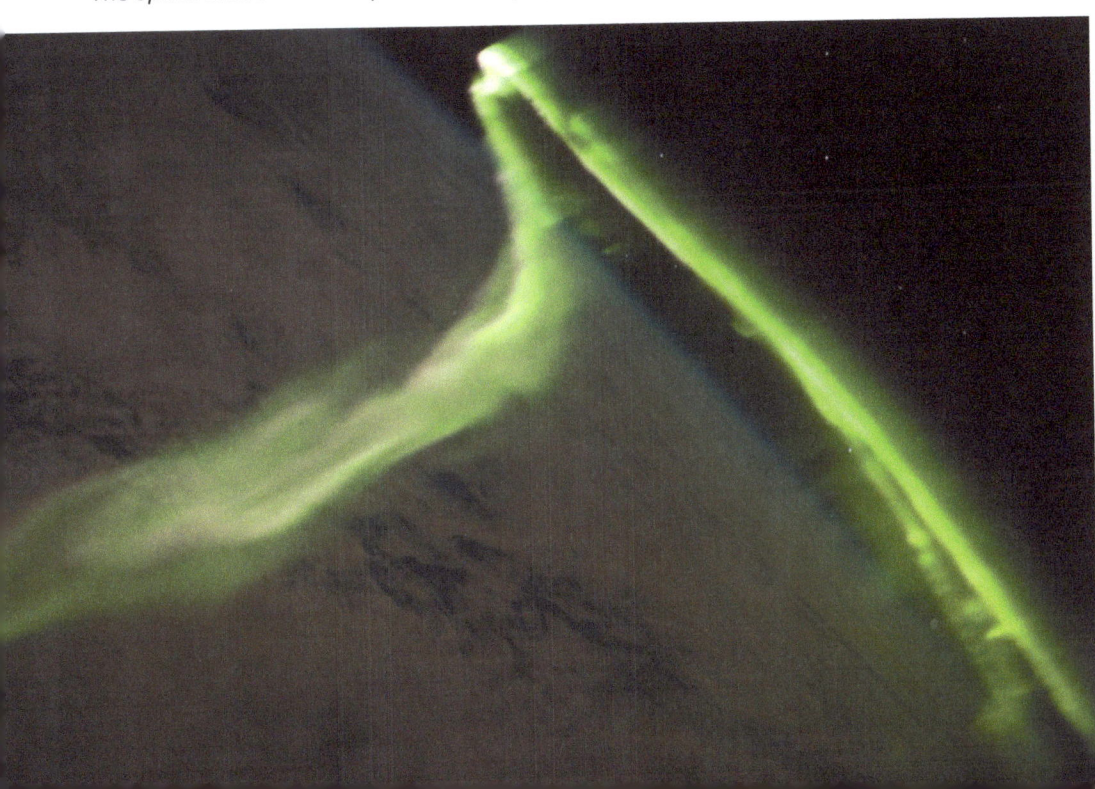

This holy Trinity, which is undivided according to its common essence but distinct according to the properties of its persons, gave the teaching of salvation to the human race through Moses and the holy prophets and his other servants, according to the most appropriate disposition of the times.

—*Fourth Lateran Council, 1215*

REVELATION TO THE PROPHETS

Old Testament prophet Job in prayer by French painter Bonnat in 1880.

God speaks to Job icon from Mount Athos, Greece, 12th c.

I BELIEVE

That besides the Canonical Scriptures nothing be read in church under the name of divine Scripture. But the Canonical Scriptures are as follows:

Genesis. Exodus. Leviticus. Numbers. Deuteronomy. Joshua the Son of Nun. The Judges. Ruth. The Kings, iv. books. The Chronicles, ij. books. Job. The Psalter. The Five books of Solomon. The Twelve Books of the Prophets. Isaiah. Jeremiah. Ezechiel. Daniel. Tobit. Judith. Esther. Ezra, ij. books. Macchabees, ij. books.

The New Testament. The Gospels, iv. books. The Acts of the Apostles, j. book. The Epistles of Paul, xiv. The Epistles of Peter, the Apostle, ij. The Epistles of John the Apostle, iij. The Epistles of James the Apostle, j. The Epistle of Jude the Apostle, j. The Revelation of John, j. book.

Let this be sent to our brother and fellow bishop, Boniface, and to the other bishops of those parts, that they may confirm this canon, for these are the things which we have received from our fathers to be read in church.

— *Council of Carthage, 419*

SACRED SCRIPTURE

Page from the Codex Vaticanus, one of the best preserved and most intact early Biblical manuscripts, beginning of 4th c.

A painting of Jacob's Ladder by Spanish painter José de Ribera, 1639.

DIVINE REVELATION

He came to a certain place and stayed there for the night, because the sun had set. Taking one of the stones of the place, he put it under his head and lay down in that place. And he dreamed that there was a ladder set up on the earth, the top of it reaching to heaven; and the angels of God were ascending and descending on it.

— *Genesis 28:11-12*

Moses went up the mountain to God. Then the Lord called to him and said, "Thus shall you say to the house of Jacob; tell the Israelites: You have seen for yourselves how I treated the Egyptians and how I bore you up on eagle wings and brought you here to myself. Therefore, if you hearken to my voice and keep my covenant, you shall be my special possession, dearer to me than all other people, though all the earth is mine. You shall be to me a kingdom of priests, a holy nation."

— *Exodus 19:3-6*

THE CALLING OF THE ANCIENT ISRAELITES

St Catherine's Monastery, in continuous use since the sixth c. AD, at the base of Mount Sinai, Egypt, the traditional site of Moses' mountain, 2008.

"Was it not necessary that the Messiah should suffer these things and enter into his glory?" Then beginning with Moses and all the prophets, he interpreted to them what referred to him in all the scriptures. As they approached the village to which they were going, he gave the impression that he was going on farther. But they urged him, "Stay with us, for it is nearly evening and the day is almost over." So he went in to stay with them. And it happened that, while he was with them at table, he took bread, said the blessing, broke it, and gave it to them. With that their eyes were opened and they recognized him, but he vanished from their sight.

— *Luke 24:26-31*

CHRIST THE WORD OF GOD REVEALS HIMSELF

'Supper at Emmaus' by Italian painter Caravaggio, 1606.

I BELIEVE

The Virgin Mary and the Infant Jesus from the catacomb of Priscilla in Rome. It is one of the oldest surviving images of its kind, 2nd or 3rd c. AD.

THE CHURCH INTERPRETS SACRED SCRIPTURE

But the task of authentically interpreting the word of God, whether written or handed on, has been entrusted exclusively to the living teaching office of the Church, whose authority is exercised in the name of Jesus Christ. This teaching office is not above the word of God, but serves it, teaching only what has been handed on, listening to it devoutly, guarding it scrupulously and explaining it faithfully in accord with a divine commission and with the help of the Holy Spirit, it draws from this one deposit of faith everything which it presents for belief as divinely revealed.

— Dei Verbum, 1965

I say that if there were a true demonstration that the sun is at the center of the world and the earth in the third heaven, and that the sun does not circle the earth but the earth circles the sun, then one would have to proceed with great care in explaining the Scriptures that appear contrary; and say rather that we do not understand them than that what is demonstrated is false. But I will not believe that there is such a demonstration, until it is shown me.

— *St. Robert Bellarmino—Letter on Galileo, 1615*

There is a link between faith and science... The Magisterium of the Church has always said so and one of the founders of modern science, Galileo, wrote that "Holy Scripture and Nature both proceed from the divine Word: one, as being dictated by the Holy Spirit, and the other, as the very faithful executor of God's orders."

— *St. John Paul II, 1979*

SACRED SCRIPUTRE AND NATURAL SCIENCE

A partial solar eclipse, 2012. Scientific discoveries have helped theologians to better understand the link between Sacred Scripture and the natural world.

In one God the Father almighty, maker of heaven and earth, of all things visible and invisible.

— *Nicene Creed*

The Nicene Creed draws its great authority from the fact that it stems from the first two ecumenical Councils... It is often more explicit and more detailed.

— *CCC 195-196*

In the beginning when God created the heavens and the earth

— *Genesis 1:1*

In the beginning was the Word, and the Word was with God, and the Word was God. He was in the beginning with God. All things came to be through him, and without him nothing came to be. — *John 1:1-3*

IN THE BEGINNING

Supernova 1994D in galaxy NGC 4526 from the Hubble pace Telescope, 1999. A supernova now visible though 50 million light years from earth.

*Vatican Observatory Telescope, Castel Gandolfo, Italy, 2008.
The Holy See has actively promoted astronomical research since the 16th c.*

WHEN WAS THE BEGINNING?

The examination of various spiral nebulae, especially as carried out by Edwin W. Hubble at the Mount Wilson Observatory, has led to the significant conclusion, presented with all due reservations, that these distant systems of galaxies tend to move away from one another with such velocity that, in the space of 1,300 million years, the distance between such spiral nebulae is doubled. If we look back into the past at the time required for this process of the "expanding universe," it follows that, from one to ten billion years ago, the matter of the spiral nebulae was compressed into a relatively restricted space, at the time the cosmic processes had their beginning.

— *Pope Pius XII, 1951*

The earth was a formless wasteland, and darkness covered the abyss, while a mighty wind swept over the waters. Then God said, "Let there be light," and there was light. God saw how good the light was. God then separated the light from the darkness. God called the light "day," and the darkness he called "night." Thus evening came, and morning followed - the first day.

— *Genesis 1:2-5*

THE SEVEN DAYS OF CREATION

Illumination of the seven days of creation, French Souvigny Bible, 12th c.

Permit me, right at the outset, to caution everyone against believing that there can be complete accuracy with respect to chronology. Indeed, we would benefit by contemplating what that wise Teacher told his acquaintances: "It is not for you to know times or seasons which the Father has fixed by his own authority" (Acts 1:7). It seems to me that Jesus, as God and Lord, delivered this succinct verdict not solely regarding the end of the world but about all times, in order to discourage those who would dare attempt such a futile undertaking.

— *Eusebius of Caesarea, 4th c.*

WISELY CHOOSING THE TOPICS WE STUDY

Royal Spanish College (14th c.) at the University of Bologna, Italy, founded in the Papal States in 1088, specializing in the study of Law, Philosophy, and Medicine. One of the oldest universities in the world. Taken in 2006.

And God said, "Let there be a dome in the midst of the waters, and let it separate the waters from the waters." So God made the dome and separated the waters that were under the dome from the waters that were above the dome. And it was so. God called the dome Sky. And there was evening and there was morning, the second day. And God said, "Let the waters under the sky be gathered together into one place, and let the dry land appear." And it was so. God called the dry land Earth, and the waters that were gathered together he called Seas. And God saw that it was good.

— *Genesis 1:6-10*

What emerges first and foremost from the progress of scientific knowledge and the inventions of technology is the infinite greatness of God Himself, who created both man and the universe. Yes; out of nothing He made all things, and filled them with the fullness of His own wisdom and goodness.

— *St. John XXIII, 1963*

CREATION REVEALS GOD'S GOODNESS

Photo of a raindrop on a fern, 2007.

When we read the inspired books in the light of this wide variety of true doctrines which are drawn from a few words and founded on the firm basis of Catholic belief, let us choose that one which appears as certainly the meaning intended by the author. But if this is not clear, then at least we should choose an interpretation in keeping with the context of Scripture and in harmony with our faith.

— *St. Augustine, 5th c.*

The question of the literary forms of the first eleven chapters of Genesis is far more obscure and complex. These literary forms do not correspond to any of our classical categories and cannot be judged in the light of the Greco-Latin or modern literary types. It is therefore impossible to deny or to affirm their historicity as a whole without unduly applying to them norms of a literary type under which they cannot be classed.

— *Pontifical Biblical Commission, 1948*

INTERPRETING THE BOOK OF GENESIS

Saint Jerome, the translator of the Bible from Hebrew and Greek into Latin and patron saint of Biblical scholars. Italian painter Caravaggio, c. 1608.

Then God said, "Let the earth put forth vegetation: plants yielding seed, and fruit trees of every kind on earth that bear fruit with the seed in it." And it was so. The earth brought forth vegetation: plants yielding seed of every kind, and trees of every kind bearing fruit with the seed in it. And God saw that it was good. And there was evening and there was morning, the third day.

— *Genesis 1:11-13*

Evolution in nature does not conflict with the notion of Creation, because evolution presupposes the creation of beings who evolve.

— *Pope Francis, 2014*

CREATION AND EVOLUTION OF PLANT LIFE

Vatican City commemorative postage stamp of Augustinian Friar Gregor Mendel who founded modern genetics in the 19th century, 1984.

IN GOD THE FATHER

And God said, "Let there be lights in the dome of the sky to separate the day from the night; and let them be for signs and for seasons and for days and years, and let them be lights in the dome of the sky to give light upon the earth." And it was so.

— *Genesis 1:14-15*

There can never, indeed, be any real discrepancy between the theologian and the physicist, as long as each confines himself within his own lines, and both are careful, as St. Augustine warns us, "not to make rash assertions, or to assert what is not known as known."

— *Pope Leo XIII, 1893*

THEOLOGY AND THE PHYSICAL SCIENCES

Galileo Galilei showing the Doge of Venice how to use the telescope, Italian painter Giuseppe Bertini, Varese, Italy, 1858.

God created the great sea monsters and all kinds of swimming creatures with which the water teems, and all kinds of winged birds. God saw how good it was, and God blessed them, saying, "Be fertile, multiply, and fill the water of the seas; and let the birds multiply on the earth."

— *Genesis 1:21-22*

The ever-flowing fountains, formed both for enjoyment and health, furnish without fail their breasts for the life of men. The very smallest of living beings meet together in peace and concord. All these the great Creator and Lord of all has appointed to exist in peace and harmony; while He does good to all, but most abundantly to us who have fled for refuge to His compassions through Jesus Christ our Lord.

— *St. Clement of Rome, 1st c.*

GOD BLESSES HIS CREATURES

Jellyfish swimming through the ocean, 2006.

Then God said: "Let us make man in our image, after our likeness. Let them have dominion over the fish of the sea, the birds of the air, and the cattle, and over all the wild animals and all the creatures that crawl on the ground."

— *Genesis 1:26*

The modern world shows itself at once powerful and weak, capable of the noblest deeds or the foulest; before it lies the path to freedom or to slavery, to progress or retreat, to brotherhood or hatred. Moreover, man is becoming aware that it is his responsibility to guide aright the forces which he has unleashed and which can enslave him or minister to him.

— *Gaudium et Spes, 1965*

MAN IN THE IMAGE AND LIKENESS OF GOD

The Prodigal Son returns to his merciful father, Dutch painter Rembrandt, 1669. This illustrates returning to the Father from the path of slavery.

God created man in his image; in the divine image he created him.

— *Genesis 1:27*

The soul not only truly exists of itself and essentially as the form of the human body... but it is also immortal.

— *Fifth Lateran Council, 1513.*

Theories of evolution which, because of the philosophies which inspire them, regard the spirit either as emerging from the forces of living matter, or as a simple epiphenomenon of that matter, are incompatible with the truth about man. They are therefore unable to serve as the basis for the dignity of the human person.

— *St. John Paul II, 1996*

THE IMMORTAL NATURE OF THE HUMAN SOUL

Unfinished sculpture of a man by Italian artist Michelangelo, Florence, Italy c. 1530

The Fine Arts are the height of human genius and reflect the depth of the artist's soul.

God male and female he created them.

— *Genesis 1:27*

But from the beginning of creation, 'God made them male and female. For this reason a man shall leave his father and mother and be joined to his wife, and the two shall become one flesh.' So they are no longer two but one flesh. Therefore what God has joined together, no human being must separate."

— *Mark 10:6-9*

THE UNION OF PROCREATION

A Human Fetus 10 weeks after conception with the amniotic sac after having been removed from the mother who had a hysterectomy, 2008. Through procreation the child is the union of mother and father.

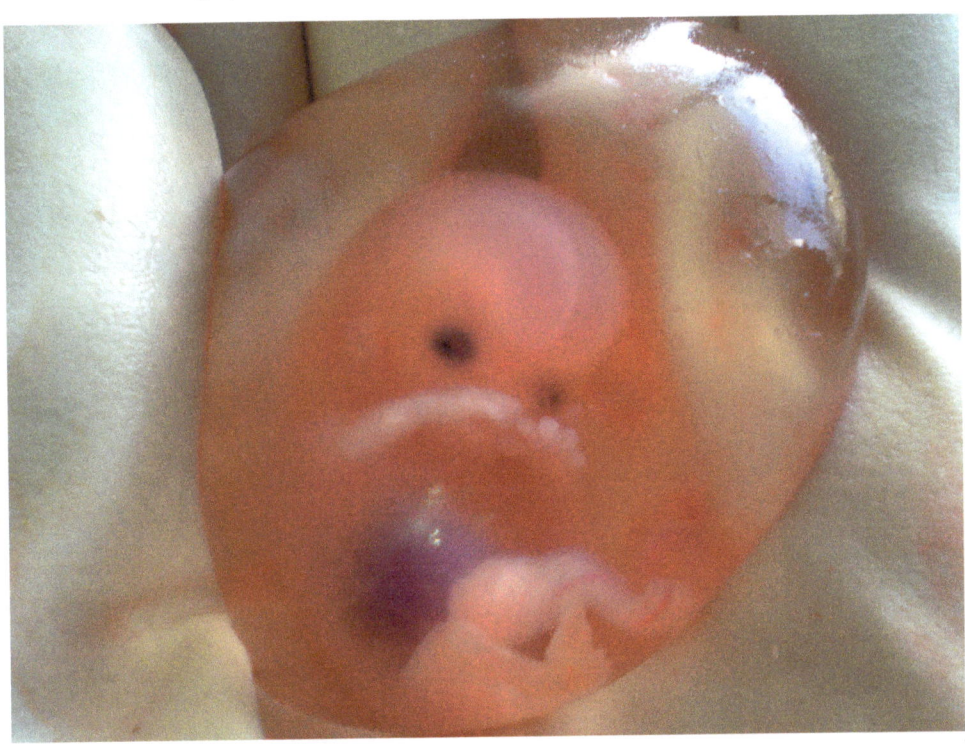

God blessed them, saying: "Be fertile and multiply; fill the earth and subdue it.
— *Genesis 1:28*

Amongst the blessings of marriage, the child holds the first place.
— *Pius XI, 1930*

The expression "subdue the earth" has an immense range. It means all the resources that the earth and indirectly the visible world contains and which, through the conscious activity of man, can be discovered and used for his ends. And so these words, placed at the beginning of the Bible, never cease to be relevant. They embrace equally the past ages of civilization and economy, as also the whole of modern reality and future phases of development, which are perhaps already to some extent beginning to take shape.
— *St. John Paul II, 1981*

GOD BLESSES HUMAN BEINGS

Salt Cathedral of Zipaquirá, 200m underground in a salt mine, Colombia, 2010.

God also said: "See, I give you every seed-bearing plant all over the earth and every tree that has seed-bearing fruit on it to be your food.
— *Genesis 1:29*

'One does not live by bread alone, but by every word that comes forth from the mouth of God.'"
— *Matthew 4:4*

FOOD FOR THE BODY AND FOOD FOR THE SPIRIT

View of fields near Vatopedi Monastery, Mount Athos, Greece, 2011. Mount Athos is a land of prayer and abundant agricultural work.

Walled Victorian Gardens, Kylemore Abbey, Connemara, Irelands, 2013

THE HUMAN VOCATION TO WORK

The Lord God took the man and put him in the garden of Eden to till it and keep it.

— *Genesis 2:15*

When he perfected this work, he gave all creation to humankind so that humans might do their work with it, in the same way that God himself had made his work, that is, humankind.

— *St. Hildegard of Bingen, 12th c.*

Labourers and craftsmen thus "maintain the fabric of the world." Developing the created world in a prudent way is the best way of caring for it, as this means that we ourselves become the instrument used by God to bring out the potential which he himself inscribed in things: "The Lord created medicines out of the earth, and a sensible man will not despise them."

— *Pope Francis, 2015*

Red Clay soil, Ultisol, 2005

THE ACCOUNT OF THE CREATION OF MAN

The LORD God formed man out of the clay of the ground and blew into his nostrils the breath of life

— Genesis 2:7

We must understand in what sense man is said to be in the image of God, and is yet dust, and to return to the dust. The former is spoken of the rational soul, which God by His breathing, or, to speak more appropriately, by His inspiration, conveyed to man, that is, to his body; but the latter refers to his body, which God formed of the dust, and to which a soul was given, that it might become a living body, that is, that man might become a living soul.

— St. Augustine, early 5th c.

And so man became a living being.

— *Genesis 2:7*

The Teaching Authority of the Church does not forbid that, in conformity with the present state of human sciences and sacred theology, research and discussions, on the part of men experienced in both fields, take place with regard to the doctrine of evolution, in as far as it inquires into the origin of the human body as coming from pre-existent and living matter - for the Catholic faith obliges us to hold that souls are immediately created by God.

— *Pope Pius XII, 1950*

THE ORIGINS OF THE HUMAN BODY AND HUMAN SOUL

Geneticist, Nobel Prize Laureate and President of the Pontifical Academy of Sciences, Werner Arber at the University of Basel, Switzerland, 2014. The Pontifical Academy of Sciences is where, encouraged by the Church, dialogue between theologians and scientists takes place.

And the LORD God planted a garden in Eden, in the east; and there he put the man whom he had formed.

— *Genesis 2:8*

Some new findings lead us toward the recognition of evolution as more than an hypothesis. In fact it is remarkable that this theory has had progressively greater influence on the spirit of researchers, following a series of discoveries in different scholarly disciplines. The convergence in the results of these independent studies—which was neither planned nor sought—constitutes in itself a significant argument in favor of the theory.

— *St. John Paul II, 1996*

HUMAN EVOLUTION

Quiver Tree Forest near Keetmanshoop, Namibia, 2012
Studies of Genetic diversity in human populations hint that modern humans originated from the San people who inhabit modern day Namibia.

Out of the ground the Lord God made various trees grow that were delightful to look at and good for food, with the tree of life in the middle of the garden and the tree of the knowledge of good and bad.

— *Genesis 2:9*

The tree of life which was planted by God in Paradise pre-figured this precious Cross. For since death was by a tree, it was fitting that life and resurrection should be bestowed by a tree.

— *St. John of Damascus, 8th c.*

THE TREE OF LIFE

Triumph of the Cross, Apse Mosaic, St. Clement's Basilica, Rome, Italy, 12th c.

The LORD God gave man this order: "You are free to eat from any of the trees of the garden except the tree of knowledge of good and bad. From that tree you shall not eat; the moment you eat from it you are surely doomed to die."
— *Genesis 2:16-17*

The Tree was, according to my theory, Contemplation, which it is only safe for those who have reached maturity of habit to enter upon; but which is not good for those who are still somewhat simple and greedy.
— *St. Gregory of Nazianzus, 4th c.*

THE TREE OF KNOWLEDGE OF GOOD AND BAD

Sixteenth c. Benedictine Abbey of Montserrat, Catalonia, Spain, 2007.
Monasteries and convents are oases of contemplation.

Naja cobra or the spitting cobra, one of Asia's most dangerous snakes, 2013. The Snake, which is feared for its venom, is the Biblical image of Satan.

SATAN THE EVIL ONE

Now the serpent was the most cunning of all the animals that the LORD God had made. The serpent asked the woman, "Did God really tell you not to eat from any of the trees in the garden?"

— *Genesis 3:1*

Eve, again, was a nest and a den for the accursed serpent, that entered in and dwelt in her. His evil counsel became bread to her that she might become dust.

— *St. Ephrem the Syrian, 4th c.*

St. Francis Borgia performing an exorcism by Spanish painter Francisco Goya, 1795. Christ the Holy One can cast out evil spirits.

THE FALL OF DEMONS

In their synagogue was a man with an unclean spirit; he cried out, "What have you to do with us, Jesus of Nazareth? Have you come to destroy us? I know who you are - the Holy One of God!" Jesus rebuked him and said, "Quiet! Come out of him!" The unclean spirit convulsed him and with a loud cry came out of him.

— *Mark 1:23-26*

For the devil and the other demons were created naturally good by God, but it is they who by their own action made themselves evil. As for man, he sinned at the instigation of the devil.

— *Fourth Lateran Council, 1215*

Now the serpent was the most cunning of all the animals that the Lord God had made. The serpent asked the woman, "Did God really tell you not to eat from any of the trees in the garden?"

— *Genesis 3:1*

Jesus said to them, "Do you not understand this parable? Then how will you understand any of the parables? The sower sows the word. These are the ones on the path where the word is sown. As soon as they hear, Satan comes at once and takes away the word sown in them.

— *Mark 4:13-15*

SATAN TEMPTS EVE

The Fall of Adam and Eve, Sistine Chapel, Vatican City, 1508-1512 by Michelangelo. With their disobedience, Adam and Eve are cast from paradise.

The woman answered the serpent: "We may eat of the fruit of the trees in the garden. It is only about the fruit of the tree in the middle of the garden that God said, 'You shall not eat it or even touch it, lest you die.'"

— *Genesis 3:2-3*

The first man, Adam, when he transgressed the commandment of God in paradise, immediately lost the holiness and justice in which he had been constituted, and through the offense of that prevarication incurred the wrath and indignation of God, and thus death with which God had previously threatened him, and, together with death, captivity under his power who thenceforth had the empire of death, that is to say, the devil, and that the entire Adam through that offense of prevarication was changed in body and soul for the worse.

— *Council of Trent, 1546*

St. Francis of Assisi by Spanish painter Francisco de Zurbarán, 1658-1664.
In his hand, he holds death, the consequence of Original Sin.

ORIGINAL SIN

The woman saw that the tree was good for food, pleasing to the eyes, and desirable for gaining wisdom. So she took some of its fruit and ate it; and she also gave some to her husband, who was with her, and he ate it.

— *Genesis 3:6*

Then they came to a place named Gethsemane, and he said to his disciples, "Sit here while I pray." He took with him Peter, James, and John, and began to be troubled and distressed. Then he said to them, "My soul is sorrowful even to death. Remain here and keep watch." He advanced a little and fell to the ground and prayed that if it were possible the hour might pass by him; he said, "Abba, Father, all things are possible to you. Take this cup away from me, but not what I will but what you will."

— *Mark 14:32-36*

THE DISOBEDIENCE OF ADAM AND THE OBEDIENCE OF CHRIST, THE NEW ADAM

Adam and Eve at the Fall, marble relief, Orvieto Cathedral, Italy, 14th c.

Then the Lord God said to the serpent: "Because you have done this, you shall be banned from all the animals and from all the wild creatures; On your belly shall you crawl, and dirt shall you eat all the days of your life. I will put enmity between you and the woman, and between your offspring and hers; He will strike at your head, while you strike at his heel."

— Genesis 3:14-15

The Virgin Mary has been designated by the holy Fathers as the new Eve, who, although subject to the new Adam, is most intimately associated with him in that struggle against the infernal foe which, as foretold in the protoevangelium, would finally result in that most complete victory over the sin and death.

— Pope Pius XII, 1950

CHRIST'S VICTORY OVER SIN AND DEATH

Fresco of the Resurrected Christ lifting Adam and Eve from the tomb above a bound Satan. St. Savior in Chora, Istanbul, Turkey, 14th c.

The man called his wife Eve, because she became the mother of all the living.

— *Genesis 3:20*

"The knot of Eve's disobedience was untied by Mary's obedience; what the virgin Eve bound through her unbelief, the Virgin Mary loosened by her faith." Comparing Mary with Eve, they call her "the Mother of the living," and still more often they say: "death through Eve, life through Mary."

— *Lumen Gentium, 1964*

MARY THE NEW EVE, THE MOTHER OF THE LIVING

Crowd in Fatima, Portugal, looking at the Miracle of the sun, which accompanied Mary's apparition and was witnessed by nearly 100,000 people, October 13, 1917. Assumed bodily into heaven, Mary has appeared to the faithful numerous times.

Mont Saint-Michel, France, whose construction was inspired in 708 by an apparition of the Archangel Michael to St. Aubert, 2014.

ANGELIC GUIDES

See, I am sending an angel before you, to guard you on the way and bring you to the place I have prepared. Be attentive to him and heed his voice. Do not rebel against him, for he will not forgive your sin. My authority resides in him.

— *Exodus 23:20-21*

Both a good and a bad angel by their own natural power can move the human imagination.

— *St. Thomas Aquinas, 12th c.*

GUARDIAN ANGELS

Italian mystic St. Gemma Galgani, who had a strong devotion to her guardian angel, 1901.

See that you do not despise one of these little ones, for I say to you that their angels in heaven always look upon the face of my heavenly Father.

— *Matthew 18:8-9*

No one walks alone, and none of us can think he is alone: this companion is always there.

— *Pope Francis, 2014*

I believe in one Lord Jesus Christ, the Only Begotten Son of God, born of the Father before all ages. God from God, Light from Light, true God from true God, begotten, not made, consubstantial with the Father; through him all things were made. For us men and for our salvation he came down from heaven, and by the Holy Spirit was incarnate of the Virgin Mary, and became man. For our sake he was crucified under Pontius Pilate, he suffered death and was buried, and rose again on the third day in accordance with the Scriptures. He ascended into heaven and is seated at the right hand of the Father. He will come again in glory to judge the living and the dead and his kingdom will have no end.

— Nicene Creed

*The Annunciation, American painter Henry Ossawa Tanner, 1898.
The moment that Christ was conceived by the power of the Holy Spirit and Mary.*

THE INCARNATION

Mary said to the angel, "How can this be, since I have no relations with a man?"

And the angel said to her in reply, "The holy Spirit will come upon you, and the power of the Most High will overshadow you. Therefore the child to be born will be called holy, the Son of God. And behold, Elizabeth, your relative, has also conceived a son in her old age, and this is the sixth month for her who was called barren; for nothing will be impossible for God."

Mary said, "Behold, I am the handmaid of the Lord. May it be done to me according to your word."

— *Luke 1:34-37*

Jesus healing a paralytic. One of the earliest surviving images of Jesus Christ, 3rd c. House Church, Dura Europos, Syria

THE MEANING OF THE INCARNATION

"I came out of paradise, I said: I will water my garden of plants." Thus speaks the heavenly cultivator, who is truly the source of wisdom, God's Word, begotten by the Father from eternity, yet remaining in the Father. In these last days, made flesh in the womb of a virgin by the operation of the holy Spirit, he went forth to the arduous work of redeeming the human race, giving himself to humanity as the model of a heavenly life.

— *Council of Vienne, 1313*

IN JESUS CHRIST

GOD BECAME MAN

5th c. Icon of Mary and Jesus 'Salus Populi Romani,' Basilica of Saint Mary Major, Rome, Italy. The image is labeled with MP θY meaning 'Mother of God.'

The Lord himself will give you this sign: the virgin shall be with child, and bear a son, and shall name him Immanuel.

— Isaiah, 7:14

It was the holy Spirit that made the virgin pregnant, but the reality of the body derived from body. As Wisdom built a house for herself, the Word was made flesh and dwelt amongst us: that is, in that flesh which he derived from human kind and which he animated with the spirit of a rational life.

— St. Leo the Great, 5th c.

The Word became flesh and made his dwelling among us, and we saw his glory, the glory as of the Father's only Son, full of grace and truth.

— *John 1:14*

We confess the Word to have been made one with the flesh hypostatically, and we adore one Son and Lord, Jesus Christ. We do not divide him into parts and separate man and God in him.

— *St. Cyril of Alexandria*

IN THE PERSON OF JESUS CHRIST THE DIVINE AND HUMAN NATURES UNITE

The actual tomb of Jesus Christ, site of his resurrection. Church of the Holy Sepulchre, Christian Quarter, Old City of Jerusalem, 2007.

One of the scribes, when he came forward and heard them disputing and saw how well he had answered them, asked him, "Which is the first of all the commandments?" Jesus replied, "The first is this: 'Hear, O Israel! The Lord our God is Lord alone! You shall love the Lord your God with all your heart, with all your soul, with all your mind, and with all your strength.' The second is this: 'You shall love your neighbor as yourself.' There is no other commandment greater than these."

— *Mark 12:28-31*

The sign that you love God, is this, that you love your fellow; and if you hate your fellow, your hatred is towards God. For it is blasphemy if you pray before God while you are angry. For your heart also convicts you, that in vain you multiply words: your conscience rightly judges that in your prayers you profit nought.

— *St. Ephrem the Syrian, 4th c.*

THE GREATEST COMMANDMENT

*St. Teresa of Calcutta helping a sick child in Calcutta, India, 1957.
She founded the Missionaries of Charity dedicated to serving the poorest of the poor.*

Abba, Father, all things are possible to you. Take this cup away from me, but not what I will but what you will." When he returned he found them asleep. He said to Peter, "Simon, are you asleep? Could you not keep watch for one hour? Watch and pray that you may not undergo the test. The spirit is willing but the flesh is weak."

— *Mark 14:36-38*

Our Lord Jesus Christ has two natures so also he has two natural wills and operations, to wit, the divine and the human: the divine will and operation he has in common with the coessential Father from all eternity: the human, he has received from us, taken with our nature in time.

— *Pope Agatho, 681*

CHRIST'S HUMAN AND DIVINE WILLS

Ancient olive trees in the Garden of Gethsemane, Jerusalem, 2008.

 IN JESUS CHRIST

A portion of the titulus crucis, brought to Rome from Jerusalem in the 4th c. and kept in the Basilica of the Holy Cross in Jerusalem, Rome, Italy, 2008.

CHRIST WAS CRUCIFIED

They crucified him, and with him two others, one on either side, with Jesus in the middle. Pilate also had an inscription written and put on the cross. It read, "Jesus the Nazorean, the King of the Jews." Now many of the Jews read this inscription, because the place where Jesus was crucified was near the city; and it was written in Hebrew, Latin, and Greek.

— John 19:18-20

Our Lord hath said: 'My yoke is sweet, and My burden light.' This burden is the cross. For if we are determined to submit ourselves, and to carry the cross this is nothing else but an earnest resolution to seek and endure it in everything for God we shall find great refreshment and sweetness therein to enable us to travel along this road, thus detached from all things, desiring nothing.

— St. John of the Cross, 1578-1579

Like water my life drains away; all my bones grow soft. My heart has become like wax, it melts away within me. As dry as a potsherd is my throat; my tongue sticks to my palate; you lay me in the dust of death. Many dogs surround me; a pack of evildoers closes in on me. So wasted are my hands and feet that I can count all my bones. They stare at me and gloat; they divide my garments among them; for my clothing they cast lots.
— *Psalm 22:15-19*

For it is better to suffer for doing good, if that be the will of God, than for doing evil. For Christ also suffered for sins once, the righteous for the sake of the unrighteous, that he might lead you to God. Put to death in the flesh, he was brought to life in the spirit.
— *1 Peter 3:17-18*

CHRIST WAS PUT TO DEATH

Pietà — Michelangelo, St. Peter's Basilica, Vatican City, 1498-1499.
One of the Sorrows of the Virgin Mary who remained ever faithful to her son.

IN JESUS CHRIST

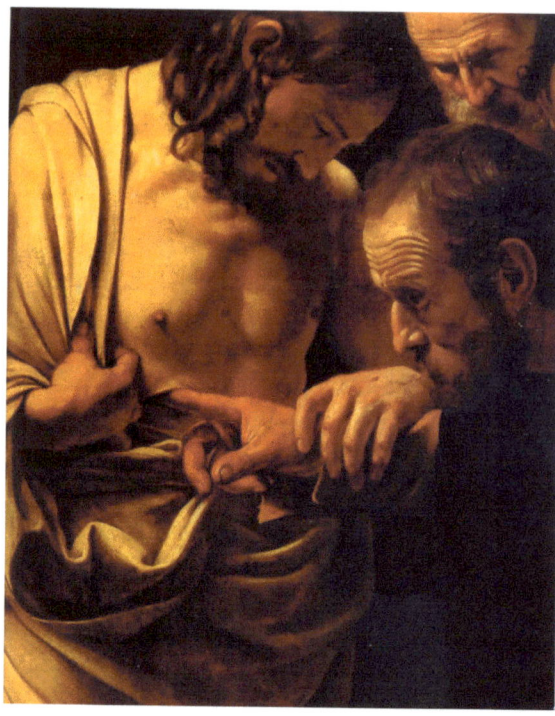

ON THE THIRD DAY HE ROSE AGAIN

'The Incredulity of St. Thomas' by Italian painter Caravaggio, 1601-1602. Doubting Thomas came to believe that Christ rose from the dead.

On the evening of that first day of the week, when the doors were locked, where the disciples were, for fear of the Jews, Jesus came and stood in their midst and said to them, "Peace be with you." When he had said this, he showed them his hands and his side. The disciples rejoiced when they saw the Lord.

— *John 20:19-20*

After His Resurrection Christ appeared in His own shape to some who were well disposed to belief, while He appeared in another shape to them who seemed to be already growing tepid in their faith.

— *St. Thomas Aquinas—13th c.*

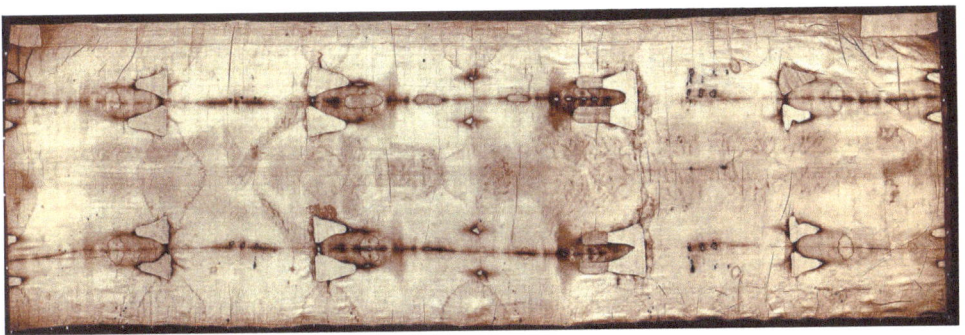

Full length photo of the Shroud of Turin. Kept in Italy since the 14th c., 2002.

When Simon Peter arrived after him, he went into the tomb and saw the burial cloths there, and the cloth that had covered his head, not with the burial cloths but rolled up in a separate place. Then the other disciple also went in, the one who had arrived at the tomb first, and he saw and believed.

— *John 20:6-8*

CHRIST'S BURIAL CLOTHS

The Sudarium of Oviedo, whose blood stains are identical to those on the Shroud of Turin. It was brought to Spain from Palestine in the 7th c., 1997.

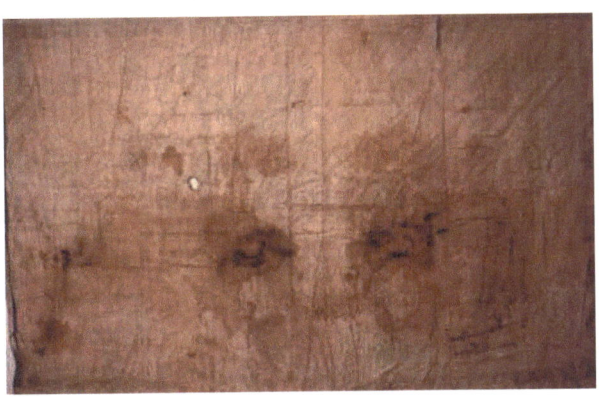

13th c. Mosaic of Christ Pantokrator, ruler of all, Hagia Sophia, Istanbul Turkey

HE IS SEATED AT THE RIGHT HAND OF THE FATHER

The LORD says to you, my lord: "Take your throne at my righthand, while I make your enemies your footstool."

— *Psalm 110*

Behold I am sending the promise of my Father upon you; but stay in the city until you are clothed with power from on high." Then he led them (out) as far as Bethany, raised his hands, and blessed them. As he blessed them he parted from them and was taken up to heaven.

— *Luke 24:49-51*

Christ the Redeemer, Rio de Janeiro, Brazil, built 1922-1931, taken 2010.

THE NEW ADAM REDEEMS HUMANITY

He was pierced for our offenses, crushed for our sins, Upon him was the chastisement that makes us whole, by his stripes we were healed.

— *Isaiah 5:3-5*

Man is born a child of the first Adam, to the state of grace and of the adoption of the sons of God through the second Adam, Jesus Christ, our Savior.

— *Council of Trent, 1547*

The Shrine of the Most Blessed Sacrament consecrated in 1999 in Hanceville, Alabama, USA, 2014.

THE BREAD OF LIFE

Jesus said to them, "I am the bread of life; whoever comes to me will never hunger, and whoever believes in me will never thirst. But I told you that although you have seen me, you do not believe. Everything that the Father gives me will come to me, and I will not reject anyone who comes to me, because I came down from heaven not to do my own will but the will of the one who sent me."

— *John 6:35-38*

The Lord Jesus Himself proclaims: This is My Body. Before the blessing of the heavenly words another nature is spoken of, after the consecration the Body is signified. He Himself speaks of His Blood. Before the consecration it has another name, after it is called Blood. And you say, Amen, that is, It is true. Let the heart within confess what the mouth utters, let the soul feel what the voice speaks.

— *St. Ambrose, 4th c.*

IN JESUS CHRIST

THE MERCIFUL CHRIST WILL COME AGAIN

The Divine Mercy image, inspired by the private revelations of St. Faustina, by Polish painter Adolf Hyła, 1943. It symbolizes charity, forgiveness, and love of God.

I saw One like a son of man coming, on the clouds of heaven; When he reached the Ancient One and was presented before him, He received dominion, glory, and kingship; nations and peoples of every language serve him. His dominion is an everlasting dominion that shall not be taken away, his kingship shall not be destroyed.

— Daniel 7:13-14

Contemplating her (Mary), assumed body and soul into heaven, we see opening up before us those "new heavens" and that "new earth" which will appear at the second coming of Christ. Here below, the Eucharist represents their pledge, and in a certain way, their anticipation.

— St. John Paul II, 2003

Last Judgement, Michelangelo, Sistine Chapel, Vatican, 1508-1512.

CHRIST WILL JUDGE THE LIVING AND THE DEAD

"Behold, I am coming soon. I bring with me the recompense I will give to each according to his deeds. I am the Alpha and the Omega, the first and the last, the beginning and the end." Blessed are they who wash their robes so as to have the right to the tree of life and enter the city through its gates. Outside are the dogs, the sorcerers, the unchaste, the murderers, the idol-worshipers, and all who love and practice deceit.

— *Revelation 22:12-15*

Yes, there is a resurrection of the flesh. There is justice. There is an undoing of past suffering, a reparation that sets things aright. For this reason, faith in the Last Judgement is first and foremost hope.

— *Pope Benedict XVI, 2007*

And in the Holy Spirit, the lord and the giver of life, who proceeds from the Father and the Son. Who together with the Father and the Son is adored and glorified: who spoke through the prophets.

— *Nicene Creed*

We also believe that the Holy Spirit, the third person in the Trinity, is God, one and equal with God the Father and the Son, of one substance and of one nature, not, however, begotten nor created but proceeding from both, and that He is the Spirit of both.

— *Eleventh Council of Toledo*

Through the centuries many professions or symbols of faith have been articulated in response to the needs of the different eras... They help us today to attain and deepen the faith of all times...

— *CCC 192-193*

It is the spirit that gives life, while the flesh is of no avail. The words I have spoken to you are spirit and life.

— *John 6:63*

The creature needs life; the Spirit is the Giver of life. The creature requires teaching. It is the Spirit that teaches. The creature is sanctified; it is the Spirit that sanctifies. Whether you name angels, archangels, or all the heavenly powers, they receive their sanctification through the Spirit, but the Spirit Himself has His holiness by nature, not received by favour, but essentially His; whence He has received the distinctive name of Holy.

— *St. Basil, 4th c.*

THE HOLY SPIRIT THE GIVER OF LIFE

A drop of water, where surface tension minimizes surface area, 2008. Water is critical compound for the proliferation of life on Earth.

These are the last words of David: "The utterance of David, son of Jesse; the utterance of the man God raised up, Anointed of the God of Jacob, favorite of the Mighty One of Israel. The spirit of the Lord spoke through me; his word was on my tongue. The God of Israel spoke; of me the Rock of Israel said, 'He that rules over men in justice, that rules in the fear of God, Is like the morning light at sunrise on a cloudless morning, making the greensward sparkle after rain."

— *2 Samuel 23:1-4*

The Holy Spirit is good, for David said: Let Your good Spirit lead me forth in the right way. For what is the Spirit but full of goodness?

— *St. Ambrose, 4th c.*

THE HOLY SPIRIT SPOKE THROUGH THE PROPHETS

Sunrise Mitzpe Ramon, Israel, 2010. Israel is the land of the Biblical Prophets.

The hand of the Lord came upon me, and he said to me: Get up and go out into the plain, where I will speak with you. So I got up and went out into the plain, and I saw that the glory of the Lord was in that place, like the glory I had seen by the river Chebar. I fell prone, but then spirit entered into me and set me on my feet, and he spoke with me. He said to me: Go shut yourself up in your house. As for you, son of man, they will put cords upon you and bind you with them, so that you cannot go out among them. I will make your tongue stick to your palate so that you will be dumb and unable to rebuke them for being a rebellious house. Only when I speak with you and open your mouth, shall you say to them: Thus says the Lord God! Let him heed who will, and let him resist who will, for they are a rebellious house.

— *Ezekiel 3:22-27*

"No prophecy of Scripture originates from private interpretation. For never by will of man was prophecy brought forth. But holy men of God spoke as they were moved by the Holy Spirit." And that Spirit who has spoken to men by the prophets is the same one who for the Apostles "opened their minds that they might understand the Scriptures" and the same who constituted his Church to announce, interpret, and preserve revelation, so that it might be "the pillar and mainstay of truth."

— *Pope Benedict XV, 1920*

Prophet Isaiah, Paris Psalter, 10th c.
He receives Divine Revelation, under
the cover of night, guided by truth.

PROPHECY IN SACRED SCRIPTURE

IN THE HOLY SPIRIT

It happened in those days that Jesus came from Nazareth of Galilee and was baptized in the Jordan by John. On coming up out of the water he saw the heavens being torn open and the Spirit, like a dove, descending upon him.
— *Mark 1:9-10*

All created nature, both this visible world and all that is conceived of in the mind, cannot hold together without the care and providence of God.
— *St. Basil, 363-364*

The site of Christ's baptism on the River Jordan, View from Qasr el-Yahud, West Bank to Churches in Al Maghtas, Jordan.

THE HOLY SPIRIT DESCENDED UPON CHRIST

When the time for Pentecost was fulfilled, they were all in one place together. And suddenly there came from the sky a noise like a strong driving wind, and it filled the entire house in which they were. Then there appeared to them tongues as of fire, which parted and came to rest on each one of them. And they were all filled with the holy Spirit and began to speak in different tongues, as the Spirit enabled them to proclaim.

— Acts 2:1-4

The fullness of the salvific reality, which is Christ in history, extends in a sacramental way in the power of the Spirit Paraclete. In this way the Holy Spirit is "another Counselor," or new Counselor, because through his action the Good News takes shape in human minds and hearts and extends through history. In all this it is the Holy Spirit who gives life.

— St. John Paul II, 1986

THE APOSTLES WERE FILLED WITH THE HOLY SPIRIT

"Cenacle" Pentecost meeting room, as restored in the 12th c., Jerusalem, 2007.

Jesus said to them again, "Peace be with you. As the Father has sent me, so I send you." And when he had said this, he breathed on them and said to them, "Receive the holy Spirit. Whose sins you forgive are forgiven them, and whose sins you retain are retained."

— *John 20:21-23*

The holy Spirit is eternally from the Father and the Son, and has his essence and his subsistent being from the Father together with the Son, and proceeds from both eternally as from one principle and a single spiration.

— *Council of Florence, 1439*

THE HOLY SPIRIT IS SENT BY THE FATHER AND THE SON

Holy Orders—Priestly ordination in the town of Schwyz, Switzerland, 2006. This Sacrament was instituted by Christ and confers the Gift of the Holy Spirit.

The Sacrament of Confirmation, French painter Nicolas Poussin, 1645.

THE HOLY SPIRIT GIVES HIMSELF AT CONFIRMATION

Now when the apostles in Jerusalem heard that Samaria had accepted the word of God, they sent them Peter and John, who went down and prayed for them, that they might receive the holy Spirit, for it had not yet fallen upon any of them; they had only been baptized in the name of the Lord Jesus. Then they laid hands on them and they received the holy Spirit.

— *Acts 8:14-17*

The beginnings of this regeneration and renovation of man are by Baptism. In this sacrament, when the unclean spirit has been expelled from the soul, the Holy Spirit enters in and makes it like to Himself. "That which is born of the Spirit, is spirit." The same Spirit gives Himself more abundantly in Confirmation, strengthening and confirming Christian life; from which proceeded the victory of the martyrs and the triumph of the virgins over temptations and corruptions.

— *Pope Leo XIII, 1897*

Now this supernatural revelation, according to the belief of the universal Church, as declared by the sacred Council of Trent, is contained in written books and unwritten traditions, which were received by the apostles from the lips of Christ himself, or came to the apostles by the dictation of the Holy Spirit, and were passed on as it were from hand to hand until they reached us.

— *First Vatican Council, 1870*

Just as Christ was sent by the Father, so also He sent the apostles, filled with the Holy Spirit. This He did that, by preaching the gospel to every creature, they might proclaim that the Son of God, by His death and resurrection, had freed us from the power of Satan and from death, and brought us into the kingdom of His Father.

— *Sacrosanctum concilium, 1963*

Bl. Gabriele Allegra a Franciscan friar who made the definitive translation of the Catholic Bible into Chinese completed in 1968, Hong Kong, 1970s.

THE HOLY SPIRIT INSPIRED SACRED SCRIPTURE

God is light, and in him there is no darkness at all. If we say, "We have fellowship with him," while we continue to walk in darkness, we lie and do not act in truth. But if we walk in the light as he is in the light, then we have fellowship with one another, and the blood of his Son Jesus cleanses us from all sin.

— John 1:5-7

A great love has been offered us, a good word has been spoken to us, and that when we welcome that word, Jesus Christ the Word made flesh, the Holy Spirit transforms us, lights up our way to the future and enables us joyfully to advance along that way on wings of hope.

— Pope Francis, 2013

THE HOLY SPIRIT LIGHTS OUR WAY

Pilgrims walking along the Camino to Santiago de Compostela, Spain, 2008.

In one, holy, catholic and apostolic church

— Nicene Creed

The communion of saints

— Apostles Creed

Painting of the Good Shepherd, Catacomb of Callixtus, Rome, mid 3rd c. This is a common figure for Christ caring for His Church.

FIGURES OF THE CHURCH

Here comes with power the Lord God, who rules by his strong arm; Here is his reward with him, his recompense before him. Like a shepherd he feeds his flock; in his arms he gathers the lambs, Carrying them in his bosom, and leading the ewes with care.

— *Isaiah 40:10-11*

The Church is a piece of land to be cultivated, the tillage of God. On that land the ancient olive tree grows whose holy roots were the Prophets and in which the reconciliation of Jews and Gentiles has been brought about and will be brought about. That land, like a choice vineyard, has been planted by the heavenly Husbandman. The true vine is Christ who gives life and the power to bear abundant fruit to the branches, that is, to us, who through the Church remain in Christ without whom we can do nothing.

— *Lumen Gentium, 1964*

St. Andrew Kim and the Korean Martyrs, 20th c. painting, Jeju Island, South Korea.

THE CHURCH IS HOLY

Christ loved the church and handed himself over for her to sanctify her, cleansing her by the bath of water with the word, that he might present to himself the church in splendor, without spot or wrinkle or any such thing, that she might be holy and without blemish.

— *Ephesians 5:25-27*

The one who granted us the light of recognizing him, the one who redeemed us from the darkness of idolatrous insanity, Christ our God, when he took for his bride his holy catholic church, having no blemish or wrinkle, promised he would guard her and assured his holy disciples saying, I am with you every day until the consummation of this age. This promise however he made not only to them but also to us, who thanks to them have come to believe in his name.

— *Second Council of Nicaea, 787*

IN THE CHURCH

THE PILGRIM CHURCH

Baldachin over the altar, St. Peter's Basilica, Vatican City, designed by Italian artist Gian Lorenzo Bernini, 1634. St. Peter's tomb, the Papal See in Rome, has been one of the main pilgrimage destinations in the history of the Church.

The Lord, however, had not chosen the people for the sake of the Place, but the Place for the sake of the people.

— *2 Maccabees 5:19*

The Church, embracing in its bosom sinners, at the same time holy and always in need of being purified, always follows the way of penance and renewal. The Church, like a stranger in a foreign land, presses forward amid the persecutions of the world and the consolations of God, announcing the cross and death of the Lord until He comes.

— *Lumen Gentium, 1964*

IN THE CHURCH

THE APOSTOLIC CHURCH

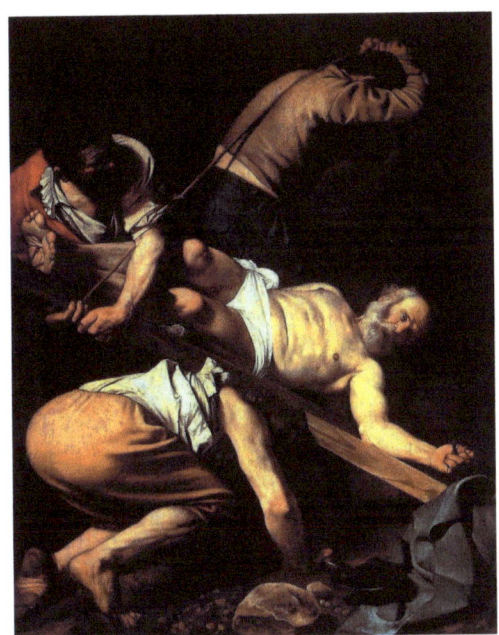

Crucifixion of St. Peter, the first of the Apostles.
Italian painter, Caravaggio, 1601.

Peter was distressed that he had said to him a third time, "Do you love me?" and he said to him, "Lord, you know everything; you know that I love you." Jesus said to him, "Feed my sheep. Amen, amen, I say to you, when you were younger, you used to dress yourself and go where you wanted; but when you grow old, you will stretch out your hands, and someone else will dress you and lead you where you do not want to go." He said this signifying by what kind of death he would glorify God. And when he had said this, he said to him, "Follow me."

— *John 21:17-19*

The very ancient, and universally known Church founded and organized at Rome by the two most glorious apostles, Peter and Paul; as also by pointing out the faith preached to men, which comes down to our time by means of the successions of the bishops. For it is a matter of necessity that every Church should agree with this Church, on account of its preeminent authority.

— *St. Irenaeus, 2nd c.*

THE ROCK ON WHICH CHRIST BUILT HIS CHURCH

Portrait of Pope Benedict XII in Avignon France, 18th c. — In 1336, he issued the Papal Bull Benedictus Deus, defining the dogma that souls of the just immediately perceive the Beatific vision upon death.

Simon Peter said in reply, "You are the Messiah, the Son of the living God." Jesus said to him in reply, "Blessed are you, Simon son of Jonah. For flesh and blood has not revealed this to you, but my heavenly Father. And so I say to you, you are Peter, and upon this rock I will build my church, and the gates of the netherworld shall not prevail against it. I will give you the keys to the kingdom of heaven. Whatever you bind on earth shall be bound in heaven; and whatever you loose on earth shall be loosed in heaven."

— *Matthew 16:16-19*

When the Roman Pontiff speaks Ex Cathedra, that is, when, in the exercise of his office as shepherd and teacher of all Christians, in virtue of his supreme apostolic authority, he defines a doctrine concerning faith or morals to be held by the whole Church, he possesses, by the divine assistance promised to him in blessed Peter, that infallibility which the divine Redeemer willed his Church to enjoy in defining doctrine concerning faith or morals. Therefore, such definitions of the Roman Pontiff are of themselves, and not by the consent of the Church, irreformable.

— *First Vatican Council, 1870*

Wood engraving of Dante's Inferno, where Dante is speaking to Pope Nicholas III committed to the inferno for simony, French artist Gustave Doré, 1861.

SCANDAL IN THE CHURCH

He said to his disciples, "Things that cause sin will inevitably occur, but woe to the person through whom they occur. It would be better for him if a millstone were put around his neck and he be thrown into the sea than for him to cause one of these little ones to sin. Be on your guard! If your brother sins, rebuke him; and if he repents, forgive him.

— *Luke 17:1-3*

For certainly no one does more harm in the Church than one who has the name and rank of sanctity, while he acts perversely.

— *St. Gregory the Great, 591*

Bl. Paul VI and Patriarch Athenagoras of Constantinople, who lifted the respective excommunications of the Great Schism of 1054, Jerusalem, 1964.

THE UNIVERSAL CHURCH

You were called as His body, it is said. You have Christ as your head; and though you were enemies, and had committed misdeeds out of number, yet has He raised you up with Him and made you to sit with Him. A high calling this, and to high privileges, not only in that we have been called from that former state, but in that we are called both to such privileges, and by such a method.

— *St. John Chrysostom, 4th c.*

The Catholic Church holds in high esteem the institutions, liturgical rites, ecclesiastical traditions and the established standards of the Christian life of the Eastern Churches, for in them, distinguished as they are for their venerable antiquity, there remains conspicuous the tradition that has been handed down from the Apostles through the Fathers and that forms part of the divinely revealed and undivided heritage of the universal Church.

— *Orientalium Ecclesiarum, 1964*

He said to them, "Go into the whole world and proclaim the gospel to every creature."

— *Mark 16:15*

There exists an admirable bond of union, such that the variety within the Church in no way harms its unity; rather it manifests it, for it is the mind of the Catholic Church that each individual Church or Rite should retain its traditions whole and entire and likewise that it should adapt its way of life to the different needs of time and place.

— *Orientalium Ecclesiarum, 1964*

THE MISSION OF THE CHURCH

Rock-hewn Church of Saint George, Lalibela, Ethiopia, 12th c. Christianity was brought to Ethiopia in the 1st c. by Philip the Evangelist and the Apostle Matthew.

The Lord said to Moses, "See, I have chosen Bezalel, son of Uri, son of Hur, of the tribe of Judah, and I have filled him with a divine spirit of skill and understanding and knowledge in every craft: in the production of embroidery, in making things of gold, silver or bronze, in cutting and mounting precious stones, in carving wood, and in every craft."

— *Exodus 31:1-5*

Very rightly the fine arts are considered to rank among the noblest activities of man's genius, and this applies especially to religious art and to its highest achievement, which is sacred art. These arts, by their very nature, are oriented toward the infinite beauty of God which they attempt in some way to portray by the work of human hands; they achieve their purpose of redounding to God's praise and glory in proportion as they are directed the more exclusively to the single aim of turning men's minds devoutly toward God.

— *Sacrosanctum concilium, 1963*

Icon of Christ Pantokrator encaustic, St. Catherine's Monastery, Egypt, 6th c.

SACRED ARTISTS

The Dwelling itself you shall make out of sheets woven of fine linen twined and of violet, purple and scarlet yarn, with cherubim embroidered on them.

— *Exodus 26:1*

The honour paid to an image traverses it, reaching the model, and he who venerates the image, venerates the person represented in that image.

— *Second Council of Nicaea, 787*

VENERATING THOSE REPRESENTED BY SACRED ART

Ceiling mosaic of the cherubim and angels, Cefalù cathedral, Sicily, 12th c.

Another man appeared, distinguished by his white hair and dignity, and with an air about him of extraordinary, majestic authority. Onias then said of him, "This is God's prophet Jeremiah, who loves his brethren and fervently prays for his people and their holy city." Stretching out his right hand, Jeremiah presented a gold sword to Judas. As he gave it to him he said, "Accept this holy sword as a gift from God; with it you shall crush your adversaries."

— *2 Maccabees 15:13-16*

The devotion based on any apparition, in as far as it regards the fact itself, that is to say in as far as it is relative, always implies the hypothesis of the truth of the fact; while in as far as it is absolute, it must always be based on the truth, seeing that its object is the persons of the saints who are honoured.

— *St. Pius X, 1907*

APPARITIONS IN THE CHURCH

The conversion of Saint Paul on the Road to Damascus, when Christ appeared to St. Paul (1 Corinthians 15:8) — Italian painter Caravaggio, 1600.

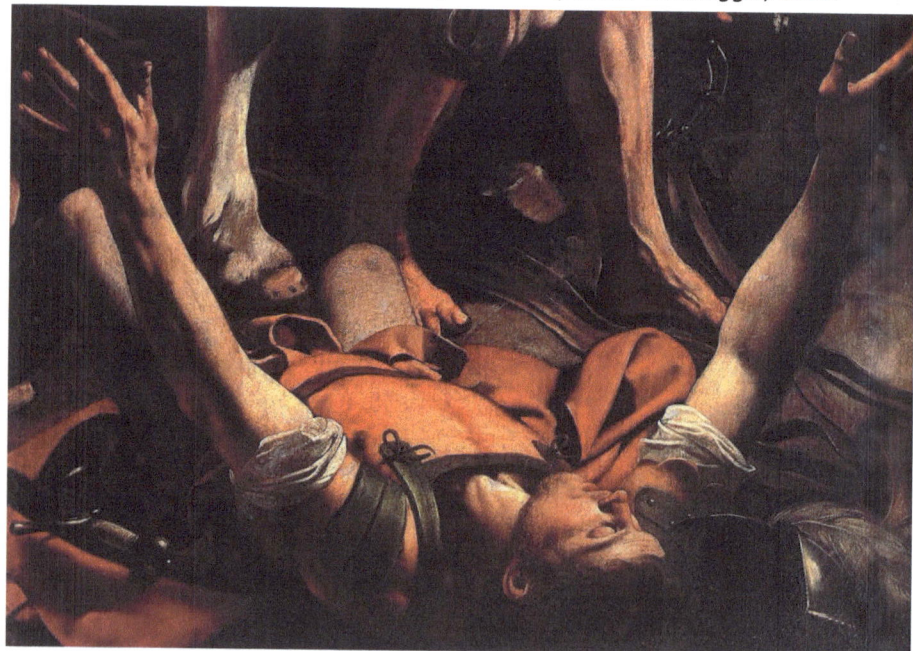

IN THE COMMUNION OF SAINTS

INTERCESSION

Photograph of the Marian apparition witness by tens of thousands of people at the Coptic Church of St. Mary in Zeitoun Cairo, Egypt, April 2, 1968.

The LORD appeared to Abraham by the terebinth of Mamre, as he sat in the entrance of his tent, while the day was growing hot. Looking up, he saw three men standing nearby. When he saw them, he ran from the entrance of the tent to greet them; and bowing to the ground.

— *Genesis 18:1-2*

The Communion of Saints, as everyone knows, is nothing but the mutual communication of help, expiation, prayers, blessings, among all the faithful, who, whether they have already attained to the heavenly country, or are detained in the purgatorial fire, or are yet exiles here on earth, all enjoy the common franchise of that city whereof Christ is the head, and the constitution is charity.

— *Pope Leo XIII, 1902*

Relics of St. Clare of Assisi, her sandal, hair and belt, 13th c. Assisi, Italy, 2006

POOR IN SPIRIT

Blessed are the poor in spirit, for theirs is the kingdom of heaven.

— *Matthew 5:3*

The holy virgins of the Second Order who participate "in the angelic life which was made known by St. Clare" by the snow-like whiteness of their souls, should continue to spread abroad, like lilies planted in the Garden of the Lord, a sweet fragrance so pleasing to God. Through their prayers, may sinners in much larger numbers hasten back to the merciful arms of Christ Our Lord, and may Our Holy Mother the Church feel the increasing joy of seeing her children restored to divine grace and to the hope of eternal life.

— *Pius XI, 1926*

SPIRITUAL COMFORT

St. Augustine and his mother St. Monica, Dutch painter Ary Scheffer, 1846.

Blessed are they who mourn, for they will be comforted.
— *Matthew 5:4*

Again, in Confessions, in the ninth book, our Saint records a conversation with his mother, St Monica... It is a very beautiful scene: he and his mother are at Ostia, at an inn, and from the window they see the sky and the sea, and they transcend the sky and the sea and for a moment touch God's heart in the silence of created beings. And here a fundamental idea appears on the way towards the Truth: creatures must be silent, leaving space for the silence in which God can speak. This is still true in our day too. At times there is a sort of fear of silence, of recollection, of thinking of one's own actions, of the profound meaning of one's life.

— *Pope Benedict XVI, 2010*

MEEKNESS

St. Juan Diego while witnessing the Guadalupe apparition of the Virgin Mary in 1531 by Mexican painter Miguel Cabrera, 18th c.

Blessed are the meek, for they will inherit the land.

— *Matthew 5:5*

Our Lady of Guadalupe, Patroness of All America, who on more than one occasion, with the tenderness of a mother, contributed to the reconciliation and integral liberation of the people of Mexico, not by the sword or force but by love and the faith. From the beginning, the "mother of the one great God of truth who gives us life", asked St Juan Diego to build a "little house" where she could give a motherly welcome both to those who are "very close" and those who are "very far."

— *Pope Francis, 2014*

Martyred statesman St. Thomas More, by German artist Hans Holbein, 1527.

RIGHTEOUSNESS

Blessed are they who hunger and thirst for righteousness, for they will be satisfied.

— *Matthew 5:6*

Saint Thomas More, who distinguished himself by his constant fidelity to legitimate authority and institutions precisely in his intention to serve not power but the supreme ideal of justice. His life teaches us that government is above all an exercise of virtue… His profound detachment from honours and wealth, his serene and joyful humility, his balanced knowledge of human nature and of the vanity of success, his certainty of judgement rooted in faith: these all gave him that confident inner strength that sustained him in adversity and in the face of death.

— *St. John Paul II, 2000*

MERCY

St. Josephine Bakhita, was kidnapped from her home in Darfur and forced to convert to Islam. Once free, she became a nun and forgave her captors. Italy, 1940s.

Blessed are the merciful, for they will be shown mercy.

— *Matthew 5:7*

Josephine Bakhita. How truly relevant she is to the Church in the Sudan today! "Hers is a message of heroic goodness modelled on the goodness of the heavenly Father. She has left us a witness of evangelical reconciliation and forgiveness, which will surely bring consolation to the Christians of her homeland."

— *St. John Paul II, 1992*

PURITY

St. Bernadette Soubirous, Lourdes, France, 1861.
She is a model for faith, holiness and purity.

Blessed are the clean of heart, for they will see God.
— *Matthew 5:8*

From February 11 to July 16, 1858, the Blessed Virgin Mary was pleased, as a new favor, to manifest herself in the territory of the Pyrenees to a pious and pure child of a poor, hardworking, Christian family. "She came to Bernadette," We once said. "She made her her confidante, her collaboratrix, the instrument of her maternal tenderness and of the merciful power of her Son, to restore the world in Christ through a new and incomparable outpouring of the Redemption."

— *Pope Pius XII, 1957*

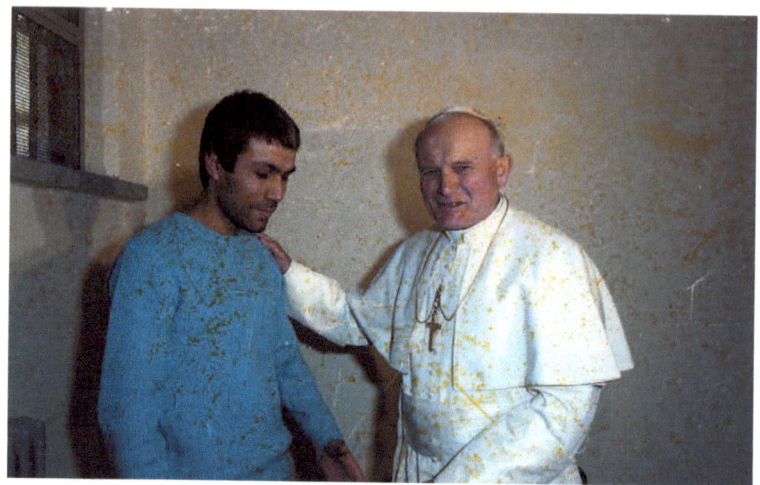

St. John Paul II forgiving his would be assassin Mehmet Ali Ağca in prison in Rome in 1983. Ağca shot him four times in Saint Peter's square, Rome in 1981.

MAKING PEACE

Blessed are the peacemakers, for they will be called children of God.
— *Matthew 5:9*

At stake is the dignity of the human person, whose defense and promotion have been entrusted to us by the Creator, and to whom the men and women at every moment of history are strictly and responsibly in debt. As many people are already more or less clearly aware, the present situation does not seem to correspond to this dignity. Every individual is called upon to play his or her part in this peaceful campaign, a campaign to be conducted by peaceful means, in order to secure development in peace, in order to safeguard nature itself and the world about us. The Church too feels profoundly involved in this enterprise, and she hopes for its ultimate success.

— *St. John Paul II, 1987*

Portrait of St. Maximilian Kolbe, Franciscan who was killed in the Auschwitz concentration camp during World War Two, 1976

COURAGE

Blessed are they who are persecuted for the sake of righteousness, for theirs is the kingdom of heaven.
— *Matthew 5:10*

In this site of the terrible slaughter that brought death to four million people of different nations, Father Maximilian voluntarily offered himself for death in the starvation bunker for a brother, and so won a spiritual victory like that of Christ himself. This brother still lives today in the land of Poland.
— *St. John Paul II, 1979*

An Egyptian Coptic Christian worker martyred in Libya for his faith, Feb. 12, 2015

MARTYRDOM

Blessed are you when they insult you and persecute you and utter every kind of evil against you falsely because of me. Rejoice and be glad, for your reward will be great in heaven. Thus they persecuted the prophets who were before you.

— *Matthew 5:11-12*

The blood of our Christian brothers and sisters is a testimony which cries out to be heard. It makes no difference whether they be Catholics, Orthodox, Copts or Protestants. They are Christians! Their blood is one and the same. Their blood confesses Christ. As we recall these brothers who died only because they confessed Christ, I ask that we encourage each other to go forward with this ecumenism which is giving us strength, the ecumenism of blood. The martyrs belong to all Christians.

— *Pope Francis, 2015*

The forgiveness of sins, the resurrection of the body, and life everlasting. Amen
> — *Apostles Creed*

I confess one Baptism for the forgiveness of sins and I look forward to the resurrection of the dead and the life of the world to come. Amen.
> — *Nicene Creed*

Chaplet of Saint Michael, 1986. Prayer aids in developing a pure heart. The chaplet of St. Michael begins with reciting the Act of Contrition.

RECONCILIATION

I tell you, all that you ask for in prayer, believe that you will receive it and it shall be yours. When you stand to pray, forgive anyone against whom you have a grievance, so that your heavenly Father may in turn forgive you your transgressions.

— *Mark 11:24-25*

The church has the mission of proclaiming this reconciliation and as it were of being its sacrament in the world. The church is the sacrament, that is to say, the sign and means of reconciliation in different ways which differ in value but which all come together to obtain what the divine initiative of mercy desires to grant to humanity.

— *St. John Paul II, 1984*

Fresco of a baptism, Catacombs of Marcellinus and Peter, Rome, c. 4th c.
This sacrament is the sacrament of spiritual rebirth.

BORN OF THE SPIRIT

Jesus answered, "Amen, amen, I say to you, no one can enter the kingdom of God without being born of water and Spirit. What is born of flesh is flesh and what is born of spirit is spirit. Do not be amazed that I told you, 'You must be born from above.' The wind blows where it wills, and you can hear the sound it makes, but you do not know where it comes from or where it goes; so it is with everyone who is born of the Spirit."

— *John 3:5-8*

Whosoever, therefore, knowing that the Catholic Church was made necessary by Christ, would refuse to enter or to remain in it, could not be saved.

— *Lumen Gentium, 1964*

IN THE FORGIVENESS OF SINS

PURE RELIGION

Roman catechumen St. Emerentiana was martyred in the great persecution of 304, being baptized by her desire and blood. Italian painting, Cortona, 18th c.

Humbly welcome the word that has been planted in you and is able to save your souls. Be doers of the word and not hearers only, deluding yourselves. But the one who peers into the perfect law of freedom and perseveres, and is not a hearer who forgets but a doer who acts, such a one shall be blessed in what he does. If anyone thinks he is religious and does not bridle his tongue but deceives his heart, his religion is vain. Religion that is pure and undefiled before God and the Father is this: to care for orphans and widows in their affliction and to keep oneself unstained by the world.

— *James 1:21-22, 25-27*

A man can obtain salvation without being actually baptized, on account of his desire for Baptism, which desire is the outcome of "faith that works by charity," whereby God, Whose power is not tied to visible sacraments, sanctifies man inwardly.

— *St. Thomas Aquinas, 13th c.*

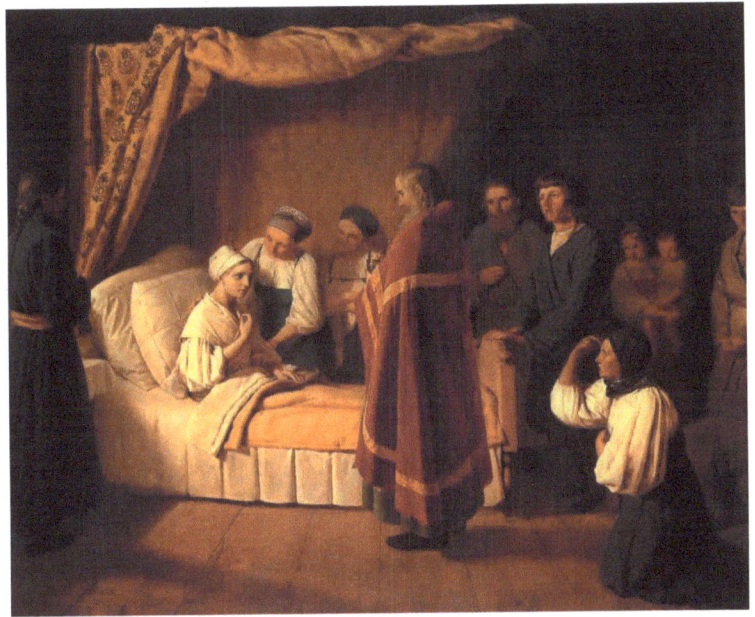

A woman receiving the viaticum or holy communion on her deathbed, Russian painter Alexey Gavrilovich Venetsianov, 1839.

THE BREAD FROM HEAVEN

Whoever eats my flesh and drinks my blood remains in me and I in him. Just as the living Father sent me and I have life because of the Father, so also the one who feeds on me will have life because of me. This is the bread that came down from heaven. Unlike your ancestors who ate and still died, whoever eats this bread will live forever."

— *John 6:56-58*

The Eucharist is to be offered to the faithful also 'as a remedy, which frees us from daily faults and preserves us from mortal sin' and they are to be shown the fitting way of using the penitential parts of the liturgy of the Mass... No one who is conscious of being in mortal sin, however contrite he may believe himself to be, is to approach the holy Eucharist without having first made a sacramental confession.

— *St. John Paul II, 1984*

Do you not know or have you not heard? The Lord is the eternal God, creator of the ends of the earth. He does not faint nor grow weary, and his knowledge is beyond scrutiny. He gives strength to the fainting; for the weak he makes vigor abound. Though young men faint and grow weary, and youths stagger and fall, They that hope in the Lord will renew their strength, they will soar as with eagles' wings; They will run and not grow weary, walk and not grow faint.

— *Isaiah 40:28-31*

As the man whom the priest baptizes is enlightened by the grace of the Holy Spirit, so does he who in penance confesses his sins, receives through the priest forgiveness in virtue of the grace of Christ.

— *St. Athanasius, 4th c.*

THE GRACE OF FORGIVENESS

Crowd waiting to say confessions to St. Padre Pio, San Giovanni Rotondo, Italy, 1967.

Amen, I say to you, whatever you bind on earth shall be bound in heaven, and whatever you loose on earth shall be loosed in heaven. Again, amen, I say to you, if two of you agree on earth about anything for which they are to pray, it shall be granted to them by my heavenly Father. For where two or three are gathered together in my name, there am I in the midst of them.

— *Matthew 18:18-20*

Having therefore, brethren, many examples of those who have sinned and repented and been saved, do also heartily make confession unto the Lord, that you may both receive the forgiveness of your former sins, and be counted worthy of the heavenly gift, and inherit the heavenly kingdom with all the saints in Christ Jesus; to Whom is the glory for ever and ever.

— *St. Cyril of Jerusalem, 4th c.*

REPENTING AND FORGIVING THOSE WHO HAVE WRONGED US

St. John Paul II during an assassination attempt where Mehmet Ali Ağca shot him four times on May 13, 1981. After the shooting the Pope said, "pray for my brother [Ağca] ... whom I have sincerely forgiven."

May the Lord grant mercy to the family of Onesiphorus because he often gave me new heart and was not ashamed of my chains. But when he came to Rome, he promptly searched for me and found me. May the Lord grant him to find mercy from the Lord on that day.

— *2 Timothy 1:16-18*

If truly penitent people die in the love of God before they have made satisfaction for acts and omissions by worthy fruits of repentance, their souls are cleansed after death by cleansing pains; and the suffrages of the living faithful avail them in giving relief from such pains, that is, sacrifices of masses, prayers, almsgiving and other acts of devotion which have been customarily performed by some of the faithful for others of the faithful in accordance with the church's ordinances.

— *Council of Florence, 1439*

MERCY FOR THE DECEASED

The Hill of Crosses near Šiauliai, Lithuania, 2006.
The hill is a place of pilgrimage, remembrance and prayer.

*Colossus of Emperor Constantine I Capitoline Museum, Rome, Italy, 4th c.
The broken statues of the emperor testify to the vanity of worldly power.
This same emperor is also remembered for his defence of Christianity.*

HEAVENLY TREASURE

Vanity of vanities, says Qoheleth, vanity of vanities! All things are vanity! What profit has man from all the labor which he toils at under the sun? One generation passes and another comes, but the world forever stays. The sun rises and the sun goes down; then it presses on to the place where it rises.

—Ecclesiastes 1:2-5

Do not store up for yourselves treasures on earth, where moth and decay destroy, and thieves break in and steal. But store up treasures in heaven, where neither moth nor decay destroys, nor thieves break in and steal. For where your treasure is, there also will your heart be.

— Matthew 6:19-21

He said to them, "Amen, I say to you, there is no one who has given up house or wife or brothers or parents or children for the sake of the kingdom of God who will not receive back an overabundant return in this present age and eternal life in the age to come."

— *Luke 18:29-30*

Life is passing, Eternity draws nigh: soon shall we live the very life of God. After having drunk deep at the fount of bitterness, our thirst will be quenched at the very source of all sweetness.

— *St. Therese of Lisieux, 1889*

ETERNITY DRAWS CLOSER FOR EACH OF US

St. Therese of Lisieux after her death in 1897, Lisieux, France

We do not want you to be unaware, brothers, about those who have fallen asleep, so that you may not grieve like the rest, who have no hope. For if we believe that Jesus died and rose, so too will God, through Jesus, bring with him those who have fallen asleep.
— *1 Thessalonians 4:13-14*

I discovered before me a much more beautiful light, and therein heard sweet voices of persons singing, and so wonderful a fragrancy proceeded from the place, that the other which I had before thought most delicious, then seemed to me but very indifferent; even as that extraordinary brightness of the flowery field, compared with this, appeared mean and inconsiderable. When I began to hope we should enter that delightful place, my guide on a sudden stood still; and then turning back, led me back by the way we came.
— *The experience of a dying man documented by St. Bede, 731*

REASON FOR HOPE

Camas lillies, Camas Prairie Centennial Idaho, USA, 2011. The natural beauty of flowers testify to God's generosity and is a symbol for His Church.

WHEN OUR WORLD COMES TO AND END

Bl. Marie-Clementine Anuarite Nengapeta who was killed by rebels in Congo's civil war. Before dying, she said to her attacker "I forgive you for you know not what you are doing." Bafwabaka, Democratic Republic of the Congo, 1964.

After a long time the master of those servants came back and settled accounts with them.

— *Matthew 25:19*

Each one, then, should think about his own passing, as holy scripture says: "In all works, be mindful of the most recent." When, therefore, any one passes away that moment is the end of his world.

— *St. Isidore of Seville, 7th c.*

Details of the face from the image of Our Lady of Guadalupe on St. Juan Diego's tilma, from an apparition of the Virgin Mary in Mexico City in 1531.

OUR OWN RESURRECTION

So also is the resurrection of the dead. It is sown corruptible; it is raised incorruptible. It is sown dishonorable; it is raised glorious. It is sown weak; it is raised powerful. It is sown a natural body; it is raised a spiritual body. If there is a natural body, there is also a spiritual one. So, too, it is written, "The first man, Adam, became a living being," the last Adam a life-giving spirit.

— *1 Corinthians, 15:42-45*

It is our hope that belief in Mary's bodily Assumption into heaven will make our belief in our own resurrection stronger and render it more effective.

— *Pius XII, 1950*

*According to tradition, the location of the Burning Bush,
St. Catherine's Monastery, Sinai, Egypt, 2011*

THE SOULS OF THE BLESSED BEHOLD GOD

God called out to him from the bush, "Moses! Moses!" He answered, "Here I am." God said, "Come no nearer! Remove the sandals from your feet, for the place where you stand is holy ground. I am the God of your father," he continued, "the God of Abraham, the God of Isaac, the God of Jacob." Moses hid his face, for he was afraid to look at God.

— *Exodus 3:3-6*

Such intuitive and face-to-face vision and enjoyment has or will have begun for these souls, the same vision and enjoyment has continued and will continue without any interruption and without end until the last Judgment and from then on forever.

— *Pope Benedict XII, 1336*

Christ Pantocrator mosaic, Hosios Loukas Monastery, Greece, 11th c.

LAST JUDGEMENT

When the Son of Man comes in his glory, and all the angels with him, he will sit upon his glorious throne, and all the nations will be assembled before him. And he will separate them one from another, as a shepherd separates the sheep from the goats.

— *Matthew 25:31-32*

For before we reign with Christ in glory, all of us will be made manifest "before the tribunal of Christ, so that each one may receive what he has won through the body, according to his works, whether good or evil" and at the end of the world "they who have done good shall come forth unto resurrection of life; but those who have done evil unto resurrection of judgment". Reckoning therefore that "the sufferings of the present time are not worthy to be compared with the glory to come that will be revealed in us.

— *Lumen Gentium, 1964*

St. Alberto Hurtado dedicated his life to serving the poor and children. Chilean postage stamp in honour of St. Alberto Hurtado, 2005.

CHARITY

And the king will say to them in reply, 'Amen, I say to you, whatever you did for one of these least brothers of mine, you did for me.'

— *Matthew 24:40*

Through charity to God we conceive virtues, and through charity toward our neighbours they are brought to birth. Being thus, loving your neighbour sincerely, without any falsity of love or heart, freely, without any regard to your own profit, spiritual or temporal. You shall be a true servant, and respond by means of your neighbour to the love which your Creator bears to you. You shall be a faithful, not a faithless bride.

— *St. Catherine of Siena, 14th c.*

SIN

The mocking of Christ, Gioacchino Asserto, 17th c.

He will answer them, 'Amen, I say to you, what you did not do for one of these least ones, you did not do for me.'
— *Matthew 25:45*

Whatever is opposed to life itself, such as any type of murder, genocide, abortion, euthanasia or wilful self-destruction, whatever violates the integrity of the human person, such as mutilation, torments inflicted on body or mind, attempts to coerce the will itself; whatever insults human dignity, such as subhuman living conditions, arbitrary imprisonment, deportation, slavery, prostitution, the selling of women and children; as well as disgraceful working conditions, where men are treated as mere tools for profit, rather than as free and responsible persons; all these things and others of their like are infamies indeed. They poison human society, but they do more harm to those who practice them than those who suffer from the injury. Moreover, they are supreme dishonor to the Creator.
— *Gaudium et Spes, 1965*

A replica of the cross erected by the Apostle Thomas in Kokkamangalam, Kerala, India during the first c. He was martyred in India soon after, 2002.

FINAL JUSTICE

Just as weeds are collected and burned up with fire, so will it be at the end of the age. The Son of Man will send his angels, and they will collect out of his kingdom all who cause others to sin and all evildoers. They will throw them into the fiery furnace, where there will be wailing and grinding of teeth.

— *Matthew 13:40-42*

Remember your ancestors who had no fear of suffering exile, imprisonment, and even death itself as they purposed to keep for themselves and you the unique gift of the true Catholic faith. For they rightly knew that not those who kill the body need be feared, but the one who is able to destroy body and soul in hell. Consequently cast all your concern on God: for He has care of you and will not allow you to be tempted beyond your ability.

— *Bl. Pius IX, 1873*

Details from the face of the crucified one on the Shroud of Turin and a positive image of the face on the right, 2014.

ETERNAL LIFE

Jesus said to them, those who are deemed worthy to attain to the coming age and to the resurrection of the dead neither marry nor are given in marriage. They can no longer die, for they are like angels; and they are the children of God because they are the ones who will rise.

— *Luke 20:34-36*

Eternity is simultaneously whole; which cannot be applied to time: for eternity is the measure of a permanent being; while time is a measure of movement.

— *St. Thomas Aquinas, 13th c.*

Khor Virap monastery in the shadow of Mount Ararat, 7th c., Armenia

HEAVEN

Lo, I am about to create new heavens and a new earth; The things of the past shall not be remembered or come to mind.

— *Isaiah 65:17*

He conceived of us and called us to life. We exist in God's thoughts and in God's love. We exist in the whole of our reality, not only in our "shadow". Our serenity, our hope and our peace are based precisely on this: in God, in his thoughts and in his love, it is not merely a "shadow" of ourselves that survives but rather we are preserved and ushered into eternity with the whole of our being in him, in his creator love. It is his Love that triumphs over death and gives us eternity and it is this love that we call "Heaven": God is so great that he also makes room for us. And Jesus the man, who at the same time is God, is the guarantee for us that the being-man and the being-God can exist and live, the one within the other, for eternity.

— *Pope Benedict XVI, 2010*

Image References

All Images are in the public domain. If not otherwise noted, they are labelled for reuse and are available on the following websites:
commons.wikimedia.org   www.wikipedia.org   www.flikr.com

2 Spello's Infiorate, Umbria, Italy. Wikipedia, 2013.
3 Spanish carrack Santa Maria. Wikimedia, Edward Hart. 1907.
4 Snow Crystal. Wikipedia, Wilson Bentley, 1902.
5 Aurora Australis Wikipedia, Mission: ISS023 Roll: E Frame: 58455, 2010.
6 (left) Job. Wikipedia, Léon Bonnat, 1880.
6 (right) God speaks to Job, Great Lavra, Mount Athos. Wikipedia, Codex B. 100, 12th c.
7 Codex Vaticanus B. Wikipedia, Bibl. Vat., Vat. gr. 1209; Gregory-Aland no. B or 03.
8 El sueño de Jacob. Wikipedia, Museo Nacional del Prado, Madrid, José de Ribera, 1639.
9 Saint Catherine's Monastery, Mount Sinai. Flickr, 2008.
10 Emmaus, Pinacoteca di Brera, Milan. Wikipedia, Caravaggio, 1606.
11 The Virgin Mary, Catacomb of Priscilla, Rome. Wikipedia, 2nd-3rd c.
12 Partial solar eclipse. Wikipedia, May 20, 2012.
14 Hubble Space Telescope-Image of Supernova 1994D (SN1994D). Wikipedia, May 15, 1999
15 Vatican Observatory Telescope, Castel Gandolfo. Wikipedia.
16 Bible de Souvigny : la creation, Bibliothèque municipale de Moulins . Wikipedia, ca. 1180
17 Collegio di Spagna, Bologna, Italy. Wikipedia.
18 Raindrop on a fern frond, Sydney, Australia. Wikipedia, June, 11 2007.
19 Jerome, Valletta, Malta. Wikipedia, Caravaggio.
20 Centenary of the death of abbot biologist Gregory J.Mendel. Wikipedia, 1984.
21 Galileo Galilei a Venezia, Villa Andrea Ponti Varese, Italy. Wikipedia, 1858.
22 Jelly. Wikipedia.
23 The Return of the Prodigal Son, The Hermitage, St. Petersburg . Wikipedia, Rembrandt, 1669.
24 The Atlas Slave. Wikipedia, Michelangelo, 1530.
25 Fetus at 10 weeks. Flickr.com, 2008.
26 The Salt Cathedral of Zipaquirá, Colombia. Wikipedia, 2010.
27 Vatopedi monastery, Mount Athos, Greece. Wikipedia, 2011
28 Victorian Gardens, Kylemore Abbey, Ireland. Wikipedia, July, 2013.
29 Ultisols. Wikipedia, 2005.
30 Werner Arber, University of Basel, Switzerland. Wikipedia, 2014.
31 Quiver Tree Forest near Keetmanshoop, Namibia. Wikipedia, 2012.
32 Apse mosaic from Basilica San Clemente in Rome. Wikipedia, 12th century.
33 Monastir/Abadia de Montserrat, Spain. Wikipedia, Bert Kaufmann, 2007.
34 Naja naja, Indian cobra. Wikipedia, Pavan Kumar, 2013.
35 Saint Francis Borgia. Wikipedia, Francisco Goya, 1795.
36 The Fall of Adam and Eve, Sistine Chapel, Rome. Wikipedia, Michelangelo, 1508-1512.
37 Saint Francis. Wikipedia, Francisco de Zurbarán, c. 1658–1664.
38 Adam and Eve marble, Orvieto Cathedral, Italy. Wikipedia, 14th c.
39 The Anastasis fresco, St. Savior in Chora, Istanbul, Turkey. Wikipedia, 2004.
40 "The Miracle of the Sun", Fatima, Portugal. Wikipedia, 1917.
41 Mont Saint-Michel, France. Wikipedia, Mathias Neveling, 2014.
42 Gemma Galgani. Wikipedia, Enrico Giannini, 1900.
44 The Annunciation. Wikipedia, Henry Ossawa Tanner, 1898.
45 Healing of the paralytic, Dura Europos, Syria. Wikipedia, 3rd c.
46 Salus Populi Romani Icon, Santa Maria Maggiore Basilica, Rome. Wikipedia, 6th c.
47 Actual Tomb Of Jesus, Church of the Holy Sepulchre, Jerusalem. Flickr, 2007.
48 Mother Teresa, Calcutta, India. Myhero.com, 1957.
49 Olive Trees, Garden of Gethsemane, Jerusalem. Wikipedia, Chad Rosenthal, 2008.
50 Titulus crucis, Santa Croce in Gerusalemme Basilica, Rome. Wikipedia, 2008.
51 Pietà, St. Peter's Basilica, Rome. Wikipedia, Stanislav Traykov, 2008.
52 The incredulity of St Thomas. Wikipedia, Caravaggio, 1601-1602.

53 The Sudarium of Oviedo. Jorge Manuel Rodríguez & Mark Guscin, 1997.
53 Shroud of Turin. Wikipedia, 2002.
54 Jesus Christ Pantocrator, Hagia Sophia, Istanbul. Wikipedia, Dianelos Georgoudis, 13th c.
55 Christ the Redeemer, Rio De Janeiro. Wikipedia, 2010.
56 Shrine of the Most Blessed Sacrament, Hanceville, Alabama. olamshrine.com, 2014.
57 Divine Mercy. Wikipedia, Adolf Hyła, 1943.
58 The Last Judgment, Sistine Chapel, Vatican. Wikipedia, 16th c.
60 A drop of water. Flikr, José Manuel Suárez, 2008.
61 Sunrise Mitzpe Ramon, Israel. Wikipedia, 2010.
62 Paris psalter (BnF MS Grec 139), folio 435v. Wikipedia, 10th c.
63 Qasr el-Yahud, West Bank and Jordan. Wikipedia.
64 Cenacle Room, Jerusalem. Flickr, Seetheholyland.net, 2007.
65 Priestly Ordination. Wikipedia, Schwyz, Switzerland, 2006.
66 Confirmation II. Wikipedia, Nicolas Poussin, 1645.
67 Venerable Gabriele Allegra. Wikipedia, 2005.
68 Camino de Santiago. Wikipedia, 2008.
70 Good shepherd, catacomb of Callixtus, Rome. Wikipedia, 3rd c.
71 Korean martyrs. Wikipedia, 20th c.
72 Baldacchino and Choir of St. Peter's Basilica, Rome. Wikipedia, 1634.
73 Martyrdom of St. Peter. Wikipedia, Caravaggio, 1601.
74 Portrait of Pope Benedict XII, Avignon, France. Wikipedia, Henri Segur, 18th c.
75 Dante speaks to Pope Nicholas III in the Inferno. Wikipedia, Gustave Doré, 1861.
76 Pope Paul VI and Patriarch Athenagoras, Jerusalem. radiovaticana.va, 1964.
77 Bete Giyorgis (Church of St. George), Lalibela, Ethiopia. Wikipedia, 12th c.
78 Christ Pantocrator, St. Catherine's Monastery, Egypt. Wikipedia, 6th c.
79 Mosaics, Cefalù Cathedral, Italy. Wikipedia, 12th c.
80 Conversion of St. Paul. Wikipedia, Caravaggio, 1600.
81 Our Lady of Zeitun, Cairo, Egypt. Wikipedia, 1968.
82 St. Claire of Assisi relics, Santa Chiara Basilica, Assisi, Italy. Wikipedia, 2006.
83 Saint Augustine and Saint Monica. Wikipedia, Jfhutson, Ary Scheffer, 1846.
84 Saint Juan Diego. Wikipedia, Boricuaeddie, Miguel Cabrera, 18th c.
85 Saint Thomas More. Wikipedia, Hans Holbein, the Younger, 1527.
86 Saint Josephine Bakhita. Communio.stblogs.org, J. Michael Thompson, 2010.
87 St. Bernadette. Wikipedia, 1861.
88 Pope John Paul II with Mehmet Ali Agca, Rome. Religionnews.com, Paul Haring, 1983.
89 Saint Maximilian Kolbe. Wikipedia, 1976.
90 Coptic Martyr, Libya. theconservativetreehouse.files.wordpress.com, 2015.
92 Saint Michael chaplet. Wikipedia, 1986.
93 Fresco of a baptism, Catacombs of Marcellinus and Peter, Rome. Wikipedia, 4th c.
94 Saint Emerentiana, Cortona, Italy. www.chiesacattolica.it, 18th c.
95 Administration of the Eucharist to a dying person. Wikipedia, Alexey Venetsianov, 1839.
96 Padre Pio in the confessional, San Giovanni Rotondo, Italy. caccioppoli.com, 1967.
97 Pope John Paul II Assassination attempt. Wikipedia, 1981.
98 Hill of Crosses, Šiauliai, Lithuania. Wikipedia, 2006.
99 Colossus of Constantine, Capitoline Museum, Rome. Wikipedia, , 2008.
100 Saint Therese of Lisieux, France. Wikipedia, parish.rcdow.org.uk, 1897.
101 Camas lilies blooming in the marsh at sunset , Idaho, USA. Wikipedia, 2011.
102 Bl. Marie-Clementine Anuarite Nengapeta, Dem. Rep. of Congo., 1964.
103 Our Lady of Guadalupe, Mexico. Wikipedia, 16th c.
104 Burning Bush, St. Catherine's Monastery, Egypt., Wikipedia, 2011.
105 Christ Pantocrator, Hosios Loukas Monastery, Greece. Wikipedia, 11th c.
106 Saint Alberto Hyrtado Stamp, Chile. www.misyononline.com, 2005
107 Mocking of Christ. Wikipedia, Gioacchino Asserto, 17th c.
108 Saint Thomas Cross, Kokkamangalam, India. Wikipedia, 2002.
109 The Shroud of Turin with digital negative. Wikipedia, 2014.
110 Khor Virap monastery and Mount Ararat, Armenia. Wikipedia, 2007.

References

Online Source Databases

The New American Bible, decrees of the Ecumenical Councils and Papal writings are available online on the following websites:
www.vatican.va   www.ewtn.com

The writings of the Fathers and Doctors of the church are available online on the following websites:
www.ccel.org   www.newadvent.org
www.tertullian.org   www.christianmind.org
www.academia.edu   opcentral.org

Sacred Scripture

Reference	Page
Genesis 1:1	14
Genesis 1:2-5	16
Genesis 1:6-10	18
Genesis 1:11-13	20
Genesis 1:14-15	21
Genesis 1:21-22	22
Genesis 1:26	23
Genesis 1:27	24, 25
Genesis 1:28	26
Genesis 1:29	27
Genesis 2:7	29, 30
Genesis 2:8	31
Genesis 2:9	32
Genesis 2:15	28
Genesis 2:16-17	33
Genesis 3:1	34, 36
Genesis 3:2-3	37
Genesis 3:6	38
Genesis 3:14-15	39
Genesis 3:20	40
Genesis 18:1-2	81
Genesis 28:11-12	8
Exodus 3:3-6	104
Exodus 19:3-6	9
Exodus 23:20-21	41
Exodus 26:1	79
Exodus 31:1-5	78
2 Samuel 23:1-4	61
2 Maccabees 15:13-16	80
2 Maccabees 5:19	72
Psalm 22:15-19	51
Psalm 110	54
Ecclesiastes 1:2-5	99
Ezekiel 3:22-27	62
Isaiah 5:3-5	55
Isaiah 7:14	46
Isaiah 40:10-11	70
Isaiah 40:28-31	96
Isaiah 65:17	110
Daniel 7:13-14	57
Matthew 4:4	27
Matthew 5:3	82
Matthew 5:4	83
Matthew 5:5	84
Matthew 5:6	85
Matthew 5:7	86
Matthew 5:8	87
Matthew 5:9	88
Matthew 5:10	89
Matthew 5:11-12	90
Matthew 6:19-21	99
Matthew 7:7-8	3
Matthew 13:40-42	108
Matthew 16:16-19	74
Matthew 18:8-9	42
Matthew 18:18-20	97
Matthew 24:40	106
Matthew 25:19	102
Matthew 25:31-32	105
Matthew 25:45	107
Mark 1:9-10	63
Mark 1:23-26	35
Mark 4:13-15	36
Mark 10:6-9	25
Mark 11:24-25	92
Mark 12:28-31	48
Mark 14:32-36	38
Mark 14:36-38	49
Mark 16:15	77
Luke 1:34-37	44
Luke 17:1-3	75
Luke 18:29-30	100
Luke 20:34-36	109
Luke 24:26-31	10
Luke 24:49-51	54
John 1:1-3	14
John 1:5-7	68
John 1:14	47
John 3:5-8	93
John 6:35-38	56
John 6:56-58	95
John 6:63	60
John 19:18-20	50
John 20:6-8	53
John 20:19-20	52
John 20:21-23	65
John 21:17-19	73
Acts 2:1-4	64
Acts 8:14-17	66
Romans 1:20	4
1 Corinthians 15:42-45	103
Ephesians 5:25-27	71
1 Thessalonians 4:13-14	101
2 Timothy 1:16-18	98
James 1:21-22, 25-27	94
1 Peter 3:17-18	51
Revelation 22:12-15	58

CLEMENT OF ROME (92-99)
Epistula ad Corinthios
20   22

LEO I (440-461)
Letter to Flavian, bishop of
Constantinople about Eutyches
(451)   46

GREGORY I (590-604)
Regula pastoralis
1.2   75

AGATHO (678-681)
Letter of Agatho   49

BENEDICT XII (1334-1342)
Ap. Constitution *Benedictus Deus*   104

PIUS IX (1846-1878)
Encyclical *Quartus Supra*
(6 January 1873)
51   108

LEO XIII (1878-1903)
Encyclical *Providentissimus Deus*
(18 November 1893)
18   21

Encyclical *Divinum Illud Munus*
(9 May 1897)
9   66

Encyclical *Mirae Caritatis*
(28 May 1902)
12   81

PIUS X (1903-1914)
Encyclical *Pascendi Dominici Gregis*
(8 September 1907)   80

BENEDICT XV (1914-1922)
Encyclical *Principi Apostolorum Petro*
(5 October 1920)
16   62

PIUS XI (1922-1939)
Encyclical *Rite Expiatis*
(13 April 1926)   82

Encyclical *Casti Connubii*
(31 December 1930)
11   26

PIUS XII (1939-1958)
Apostolic Constitution *Munificentissimus Deus*
(1 November 1950)
39   39
42   103

Encyclical *Humani generis*
(12 August 1950)
36   30

Encyclical *Le pelerinage de Lourdes*
(2 July 1957)
10   87

Discourse
(22 November 1951)   15

JOHN XXIII (1958-1963)
Encyclical *Pacem in terris*
(11 April 1963)
3   18

JOHN PAUL II (1978-2005)
Encyclical *Laborem Exercens*
(14 September 1981)
4   26

Ap. Exhortation *Reconciliatio et Paenitentia*
(2 December 1984)
11   92
27   95

Encyclical *Dominum et Vivificantem*
(18 May 1986)
64   64

Encyclical *Sollicitudo rei socialis*
(30 December 1987)
47   88

Apostolic Letter *E sancti Thomae Mori*
(31 October 2000)
4   85

Encyclical *Ecclesia de Eucharistia*
(17 April 2003)
62   57

Discourses
(30 March 1979)   12

(7 June 1979)   89

(2 October 1992)   86

(22 October 1996)   24, 31

BENEDICT XVI (2005-2013)
Encyclical *Spe Salvi*
(30 November 2007)
43   58

Discourse
(15 August 2010)   110
(25 August 2010)   83

FRANCIS (2013-)
Encyclical *Lumen Fidei*
(June 29 2013)
7   68

Encyclical *Laudato Sii'*
(24 May 2015)
124   28

Discourses
(19 May 2014)   84
(2 October 2014)   42
(27 October 2014)   20
(16 February 2015)   90

Ecumenical Councils

EPHESUS (431)
Third Letter of Cyril to Nestorius   47

CHALCEDON (451)
Letter of Pope Leo   46

CONSTANTINOPLE III (680-681)
Letter of Agatho   49

NICAEA II (787)
Definition   71, 79

LATERAN IV (1215)
Constitutions
1   6, 35

VIENNE (1311-1312)
Decrees
38   45

FLORENCE (1439-1445)
Session 6   65, 98

LATERAN V (1512-1517)
Session 8   24

TRENT (1545-1563)
Session 5
1   37
Session 7
Decree concerning justification   55

VATICAN I (1869-1870)
Session 3 Chapter 2.5   67
Session 4 Chapter 4.9   74

VATICAN II (1962-1965)
Sacrosanctum Concilium
(4 December 1963)
6   67
122   78

Lumen gentium
(21 November 1964)
6   70
8   72
14   93
48   105
56   40

Orientalium ecclesiarum
(21 November 1964)
1   76
2   77

Dei Verbum
(18 November 1965)
10   11

Gaudium et spes
(7 December 1965)
9   23
27   107
36   5

Local Councils

CARTHAGE (419)
Canon 24   7

TOLEDO XI (675)   59

Creeds
Apostles' Creed   1, 69, 91

Toledo XI Symbol of Faith   59

Niceno-Constantinopolitan Creed   13, 43,
                                        59, 69, 91

Ecclesiastical Documents

Catechism of the Catholic Church
(11 October 1992)
192-193   59
194   1
195-196   13

Pontifical Biblical Commission
Regarding the sources of the Pentateuch and the historical value of Genesis 1-11
(January 16, 1948)   19

Doctors of the Church

Ambrose, St (339-397)
De spiritu sancto
72   61

De mysteriis
54   56

Athanasius of Alexandria, St (295-373)
Frag. Contra Navatus   96

Augustine, St (354-430)
De civitate Dei
13.24   29

De Genesi ad litteram
1.21.41   19

De utilitate credenda
30   3

Basil, St (ca. 339-379)
Liber de spiritu sancto
19   63

Epistulae
159   60

Bede the Venerable, St (ca. 672-735)
Historia ecclesiastica gentis Anglorum
5.12   101

Catherine of Siena, St (1347-1380)
Lettera a una mantellata di Santo Domenico chiamata Caterina di Scetto   106

Cyril of Alexandria, St (ca. 376-444)
Third Letter of Cyril to Nestorius   47

Cyril of Jerusalem, St (ca. 313-386)
Catecheses
2.20   97

Ephrem the Syrian, St (ca. 306-373)
Hymni de Nativitate
12   34

Sermo de Admonitione et Poenitentia
4   48

Frances de Sales, St (1567-1622)
Introduction à la vie dévote   2

Gregory the Great, St (ca. 540-604)
Regula pastoralis
1.2   75

Gregory of Nazianzus, St (ca. 330-390)
Orationes
45.8   33

Hildegard of Bingen, St (1098-1179)
Liber Divinorum Operum
1.1   28

Isidore of Seville, St (ca. 560-636)
Chronicon
122   102

John of the Cross, St (1542-1591)
Subida del Monte Carmelo
2.7   50

John Chrysostom, St (354-407)
Homiliae in ad Ephesios
Homily 9   76

John of Damascus, St (ca. 645-750)
De fide orthodoxa
4.11   32

Leo the Great, St (ca. 400-461)
Letter to Flavian, bishop of Constantinople about Eutyches   46

Robert Bellarmino, St (1542-1621)
Lettera a Paolo A. Foscarini   12

Thérèse of Lisieux, St (1873-1897)
Lettres à sa soeur Céline, V   100

Thomas Aquinas, St (ca. 1224-1274)
Summa theologiae
I,111,3   41
I,10,4   109
III, 55, 4   52
III, 68, 2   94

Other Fathers of the Church

Agatho, St (d. 691)
Letter of Agatho   49

Clement of Rome, St (d. 99)
Epistula ad Corinthios
20   22

Irenaeus of Lyons, St (ca. 140-202)
Adversus haereses
3.3.2   73

Eusebius of Caesarea (d. ca. 340)
Chronographia
1   17

Ecclesiastical Heritage

Sacred Art

Anonymous (c. 2nd – 3rd century) *Fresco of the Virgin and Child*	11
Anonymous (3rd century) *Good shepherd*	70
Anonymous (3rd century) *Jesus healing a paralytic*	45
Anonymous (4th century) *Fresco of a baptism*	93
Anonymous (5th century) *Salus Populi Romani Icon*	46
Anonymous (6th century) *Icon of Christ Pantokrator*	78
Anonymous (10th century) *Prophet Isaiah, Paris Psalter*	62
Anonymous (11th century) *Pantokrator Mosaic Hosios Loukas*	105
Anonymous (12th century) *Apse Mosaic, St. Clement's*	32
Anonymous (12th century) *Icon of Job*	6
Anonymous (12th century) *Illumation, Souvigny Bible*	16
Anonymous (12th century) *Mosaic of cherubim, Cefalù*	79
Anonymous (1261) *Pantokrator Mosaic H. Sophia*	54
Anonymous (14th century) *Resurrection, St. Savior in Chora*	39
Anonymous (14th century) *Marble relief of Adam and Eve*	38
Anonymous (18th century) *Saint Emerentiana*	94
Anonymous (18th century) *Portrait of Pope Benedict XII*	74
Anonymous (20th century) *Korean Martyrs*	71
Anonymous (20th century) *Saint Maximilian Kolbe*	89
Asserto, Gioacchino (1600-1649) *Mocking of Christ*	107
Bernini, Gian Lorenzo (1598-1680) *Baldachin, St. Peter's, Rome*	72
Bertini, Giuseppe (1825-1898) *Galileo and the Doge of Venice*	21
Bonnat, Leon (1833-1922) *The Prophet Job*	6
Buonarroti, Michelangelo (1475-1564)	
Fall of Adam and Eve	36
Last Judgement	58
Pietà	51
Unfinished Statue of Atlas Slave	24
Cabrera, Miguel (1695-1768) *Saint Juan Diego*	84
Caravaggio, Michelangelo Merisi (c. 1571-1610)	
Conversion of St. Paul	80
Crucifixion of St. Peter	73
The incredulity of St Thomas	52
Saint Jerome	19
Supper at Emmaus	10
Doré, Gustave (1832-1883) *Engraving of Dante's Inferno*	75
Goya, Francisco (1746-1828) *Exorcism by St. Francis Borgia*	35
Holbein, Hans (c. 1497-1543) *Saint Thomas More*	85
Hyła, Adolf (1897-1965) *Divine Mercy*	57

Poussin, Nicolas (1594-1665) *The Sacrament of Confirmation*	66
Ribera, José (1591-1652) *Jacob's Ladder*	8
Scheffer, Ary (1795-1858) *St. Augustine and St. Monica*	83
Tanner, Henry Ossawa (1859-1937) *The Annunciation*	44
Van Rijn, Rembrandt Harmenszoon (1606-1669) *The Prodigal Son*	23
Venetsianov, Alexey (1780-1847) *Viaticum*	95
Zurbarán, Francisco (1598-1664) *St. Francis of Assisi*	37

History and Cultural Heritage of the Church

Allegra, Gabriele Bl.	67
Arber, Werner, President of the Pontifical Academy of Sciences	30
Bakhita, Josephine, St.	86
Burning Bush	104
Cenacle Room, Jerusalem	64
Chaplet of Saint Michael	92
Clare of Assisi, St., Relics	82
Colossus of Constantine I	99
Coptic Martyr	90
Codex Vaticanus	7
Galgani, Gemma St	42
Garden of Gethsemane, Jerusalem	49
Holy Sepulchre, Jerusalem	47
Hurtado, Alberto, St. Chilean stamp	106
Infiorate, Spello, Italy	2
John Paul II, St. Assassination attempt	97
John Paul II, St. with Ali Ağca	88
Mendel, Gregor on Vatican stamp	20
Miracle of the Sun, Fatima, Portugal	40
Nengapeta, Marie-Clementine, Bl.	102
Ordination, Schwyz, Switzerland	65
Our Lady of Guadalupe	103
Our Lady of Zeitoun Apparition, Cairo, Egypt	81
Padre Pio, St. Hearing Confession	96
Paul VI, Bl. and Patriarch Athenagoras Jerusalem	76
Replicas of Christopher Columbus' Ship the Santa Maria	3
River Jordan, Al Maghtas, Jordan	63
Royal Spanish College, Bologna, Italy	17
Shroud of Turn	53, 109
Soubirous, Bernadette, St.	87
Sudarium of Oviedo	53
Teresa in Calcutta, St.	48
Therese of Lisieux, St.	100
Titulus Crucis, Church of the Holy Cross Rome, Italy	50
Vatican Observatory	15

Sacred Places		Natural Wonders	
Al Maghtas, Baptism Site, Jordan World Heritage Site	63	Aurora Australis from outer space	5
Camino de Santiago, Spain World Heritage Site	68	Camas Lilies, Idaho, USA	101
Cefalù Cathedral, Cefalù, Italy World Heritage Site	79	Drop of Water	60
Christ the Redeemer, Rio de Janeiro, Brazil, World Heritage Site	55	Human Fetus	25
Jerusalem, Old City, World Heritage Site	47, 49, 64	Jellyfish	22
Cross of Saint Thomas, Kerala, India	108	Kylemore Abbey Garden, Ireland	28
The Hill of Crosses, Šiauliai, Lithuania	98	Mount Athos, Greece	27
Khor Virap monastery, Armenia	110	Naja Cobra	34
Mont Saint-Michel, Normandy, France World Heritage Site	41	Quiver Tree Forest, Namibia	31
Mouth Athos, Greece World Heritage Site	27	Raindrop	18
Saint Catherine's Monastery, Egypt World Heritage Site	9, 104	Red Clay Soil	29
Saint Clement's Basilica, Rome, Italy World Heritage Site	32	Snowflake under a microscope	4
Saint George's Church, Lalibela, Ethiopia, World Heritage Site	77	Solar eclipse	12
Saint Peter's Basilica, Vatican City World Heritage Site	72	Sunrise Mitzpe Ramon, Israel	61
Salt Cathedral of Zipaquirá, Colombia	26	Supernova 1994D	14
Santa Maria de Montserrat Abbey Catalonia, Spain	33		
Shrine of the Most Blessed Sacrament Hanceville, USA	56		

Subject Index

Angels	41-42
Apparitions	80
Baptism, Sacrament of	93-94
Beauty of Creation	4
The Beginning of Time and Space	14-15
Burial Clothes of Jesus Christ	53
Charity	48, 106
The Church, Apostolic	73
Holy	71
Metaphors for	70
Mission of	77
Pilgrim Church	72
Scandal in	75
The Teaching Authority of	11
Universal	76
Communion of the Saints	81
Confession	96
Confirmation, Sacrament of	66
Contemplation	33
Courage	89
Creation, The Seven Days of	16-17
Creation of Man	29-31
Cross	32, 50
Crucifixion	50-51
Death	100, 102
Demons	35
Devotion	2
Divine Revelation	8, 10
The End of Our World	102
Eternal Life	109
Eternity	100, 109
Eucharist	56, 95
Evolution	20, 30-31
The Father, Blesses his Creatures	22
Blesses Human Beings	26
Creator of the Universe	14-15
Goodness	18
Food	27
Forgiveness	96-97
Genesis, Book of	19
God's Goodness	18
The Greatest Commandment	48
Guardian Angels	42
Heaven	99, 104, 109-110
Hell	108
Holy Spirit, Filled the Apostles	64
Giver of Life	60
Inspired Sacred Scripture	67
Lights our Way	68
Procession of	65
Holy Orders, Sacrament of	65
Hope	101
Human Origins	30
Human Soul	24, 30
Image and Likeness of God	23
Incarnation	44-47, 49
Intercession	81, 98
Israelites	9, 61
Jesus Christ, Baptism	63
Bread of Life	56
Human & Divine Wills	49
Merciful	57
Ruler of All	54
Second Coming	57
Word of God	10, 44-47
Justice	108
Last Judgement	58, 105
Marian Apparitions	40, 81, 103
Martyrdom	89-90
Meekness	84
Mercy	86, 98
The New Adam	38-39, 55
The New Eve	39-40
Original Sin	36-38
Papal Authority	73-74
Peacemaking	88
Penance, Sacrament of	66
Pentecost	64
Physical Sciences	21
Prayer	92
Procreation	25
Prophecy	62
Prophets	6, 61-62
Purgatory	98
Purity	87, 94
Redemption	39, 55
Reconciliation	92
Repenting	97
Resurrection of Christ	47, 52
Resurrection of the Dead	103
Righteousness	85
Sacred Art	78-79
Sacred Scripture	7, 11-12, 62, 67
Saint Peter's Authority	73-74
Satan	34-36
Scientific Investigation	5, 12, 17, 21
Sorrows of the Virgin Mary	51
Seeking the Unknown	3
Sin	107
Spiritual Comfort	83
Spiritual Poverty	82
Suffering	108
The Tree of Knowledge	33
The Tree of Life	32
University	17
Vanity of Worldly Gain	99
Water	60
Work	28

www.ingramcontent.com/pod-product-compliance
Lightning Source LLC
Chambersburg PA
CBHW042058290426
44113CB00001B/10